VSAM Guide to Optimization and Design

Books and Training Products From QED

DATABASE

Data Analysis: The Key to Data Base Design
The Data Dictionary: Concepts and Uses
DB2: The Complete Guide to Implementation and Use
Logical Data Base Design
DB2 Design Review Guidelines
DB2: Maximizing Performance of Online Production Systems
Entity-Relationship Approach to Logical Data Base Design
How to Use ORACLE SQL*PLUS
ORACLE: Building High Performance Online Systems
Embedded SQL for DB2: Application Design and Programming
SQL for dBASE IV
Introduction to Data and Activity Analysis
ORACLE Design Review Guidelines
Using DB2 to Build Decision Support Systems
How to Use SQL for DB2

SYSTEMS ENGINEERING

Handbook of Screen Format Design
Managing Projects: Selecting and Using PC-Based Project Management Systems
The Complete Guide to Software Testing
A User's Guide for Defining Software Requirements
A Structured Approach to Systems Testing
Practical Applications of Expert Systems
Expert Systems Development: Building PC-Based Applications
Storyboard Prototyping: A New Approach to User Requirements Analysis
The Software Factory: Managing Software Development and Maintenance
Data Architecture: The Information Paradigm
Advanced Topics in Information Engineering

MANAGEMENT

CASE: The Potential and the Pitfalls
Strategic and Operational Planning for Information Services
The State of the Art in Decision Support Systems
The Management Handbook for Information Center and End-User Computing
Disaster Recovery: Contingency Planning and Program Analysis

MANAGEMENT (cont'd)

Winning the Change Game
Information Systems Planning for Competitive Advantage
Critical Issues in Information Processing Management and Technology
Developing the World Class Information Systems Organization
The Technical Instructor's Handbook: From Techie to Teacher
Collision: Theory vs. Reality in Expert System
How to Automate Your Computer Center: Achieving Unattended Operations
Ethical Conflicts in Information and Computer Science, Technology, and Business

DATA COMMUNICATIONS

Data Communications: Concepts and Solutions
Designing and Implementing Ethernet Networks
Network Concepts and Architectures
Open Systems: The Guide to OSI and its Implementation
VAX/VMS: Mastering DCL Commands and Utilities

PROGRAMMING

VSAM Techniques: Systems Concepts and Programming Procedures
How to Use CICS to Create On-Line Applications: Methods and Solutions
DOS/VSE/SP Guide for Systems Programming: Concepts, Programs, Macros, Subroutines
Systems Programmer's Problem Solver
VSAM: Guide to Optimization and Design
MVS/TSO: Mastering CLISTS
MVS/TSO: Mastering Native Mode and ISPF
VAX/VMS: Mastering DCL Commands and Utilities

SELF-PACED TRAINING

SQL as a Second Language
Building Online Production Systems with DB2 (Video)
Introduction to UNIX (CBT)
Building Production Applications with ORACLE (Video)

VSAM
Guide to Optimization and Design

Eugene S. Hudders

QED Information Sciences, Inc.
Wellesley, Massachusetts

P.O. Box 82-181
Wellesley, MA 02181

Library of Congress Catalog Number: 89-24220
International Standard Book Number: 0-89435-314-4

Printed in the United States of America
90 91 92 10 9 8 7 6 5 4 3 2 1

Library of Congress Cataloging-in-Publication Data

Hudders, Eugene S.
VSAM: guide to optimization and design / Eugene S. Hudders.
p. cm.
Includes bibliographical references.
ISBN 0-89435-314-4
1. Virtual computer systems. 2. Data structures (Computer science) I. Title.
QA76.9.V5H83 1990
005.4'3--dc 20

To Nelly and Eugene who gave me of their time and encouragement to write this book.

Table of Contents

List of Figures

Preface

This book deals with the optimization and dataset design using IBM's Virtual Storage Access Method, or VSAM, as it is most commonly called. It is based on the author's experience in performing optimization studies for customers. Although the book is not meant to be an introductory course in VSAM, Chapter 1 addresses and reviews VSAM fundamentals such as terminology and concepts. A user familiar with VSAM can skim over this chapter or skip it, if so desired. Users new to VSAM may want to review this chapter as many references made in the book are covered here.

Chapter 2 is the first chapter dedicated to the optimization of VSAM. It deals with three very important and related areas that can have an important bearing on the performance of the dataset. This chapter reviews the data and index size and their relationship to the physical record size. The effect of a good CI (Control Index) selection is reviewed in detail and the effects of a poor CI selection on performance.

Chapter 3 goes into details of free space. The advantages and disadvantages are discussed. The information provided can help the user determine the free space allowance to be allocated to the different datasets in the installation. In addition, the very important topic of reorganization is discussed with its effect on the amount of free space to be allocated.

Chapter 4 is a continuation of Chapter 3 because the topic of splits (CI/CA) is closely related to the amount of free space allocated to the dataset. The negative effects of splits are discussed in detail.

Chapter 5 reviews the importance of the correct selection of the Control Area size and its effect on KSDS organization. The relationship between the number of index levels and the CA size is reviewed.

Chapter 6 discusses I/O buffer allocation. The different types of buffer allocations and when each should be specified are covered. The positive and negative effects of VSAM buffering are also reviewed.

Chapter 7 reviews the different alternatives available to the user in allocating special areas to a dataset to improve performance. Many options regarding the definition of indices are available to the user.

Chapter 8 reviews these options and discusses their pros and cons.

Chapter 9 addresses online access to data. CICS/VS and VSAM are discussed in great detail. Proper buffering and allocation techniques are reviewed. Some online programming techniques are also discussed as well as the relationship between the File Control Table and its associated operands with VSAM processing.

Chapter 10 summarizes miscellaneous areas associated with VSAM that can have an impact on VSAM performance. Different topics are reviewed and recommendations made.

Chapter 11 summarizes different problems that may prod the user toward optimizing VSAM datasets. The problems are discussed and possible solutions given for the user to investigate. The user is also referred to individual chapters in the book for additional information.

Each of the chapters and associated major sections ends with a series of recommendations, which the user can evaluate in his or her environment.

The author wishes to express his appreciation to everyone who provided ideas and helped in the preparation of this book. In particular, the author would like to thank Chris Sanchez and Julio Rivera, systems programmers at Banco de Pance in Puerto Rico, for providing input for this book.

We wish you much success in your optimization tasks, which we expect to be challenging as well as fun.

Chapter 1
VSAM REVIEW

This chapter reviews the basic VSAM structure and terminology that is used in the rest of the book. The reader can use this chapter as a brief refresher of VSAM concepts and facilities.

VSAM CONCEPTS AND FACILITIES

This chapter establishes a common terminology regarding VSAM concepts and facilities. A reader familiar with VSAM may skip to Chapter 2 where the discussion of VSAM begins.

This chapter describes the different organizations available to the VSAM user. Most of the chapter is dedicated to the key sequence organization (KSDS), which is where the main thrust of VSAM dataset tuning is performed. As this is a brief review, it is assumed that the reader is familiar with VSAM datasets and terminology.

Types of VSAM Datasets

VSAM dataset can be organized in four ways:

- Entry Sequence Dataset (ESDS)
- Key Sequence Dataset (KSDS)
- Relative Record Dataset (RRDS)
- Linear Dataset (LDS)

Each of these organizations was implemented to address different access techniques. Whenever the term "sequential" is discussed, we must differentiate between "logical" and "physical" sequential. Physical sequential processing involves the reading or writing of a dataset in the order in which the records reside on the input/output device. That is, a physical sequential dataset is read one physical block at a time without considering whether or not the data is in any logical (ascending or descending) record sequence. This means that the dataset may or may not be in collating sequence such as by social security or employee number. The first block read would be block number 1, followed by block number 2, followed by block number 3, and so on. Each subsequent block read is one greater than the previous block number. A physical sequential file can also be in logical sequence, but it will be processed in a physical sequential manner.

A dataset read in logical sequence means that the data is to be processed in a particular collating sequence (ascending or descending) such as by social security number. In this case, the user created the dataset in a particular identified collating sequence by a specified key or control field. A dataset organized in a logical sequence is processed in this order, which may or may not be in physical sequence. Another method of accessing a dataset is direct. In this method, the user is able to identify the desired record and access this record without having to access or read any other data record in the file. One final method of accessing a dataset is a combination of direct and sequential processing. In this method, the user can access a particular record and then optionally continue to process sequentially.

The user selects the actual organization, depending on the particular use that is to be given to the dataset. For example, if the user is interested in having a file that is to be processed sequentially with little or no regard to its logical sequence, an ESDS organization can be used. ESDS allows records to be processed in physical sequence regardless of the logical sequence. If the user is interested in obtaining a record directly without having to read through the dataset, an RRDS organization can be used. The RRDS organization allows the user to go directly to the record by using a relative position identifier which permits access to the desired record without having to read sequentially through the dataset. Depending on the algorithm used to determine the record's location, the accessing of an RRDS dataset in a logical sequence may be inefficient. If the user desires a dataset that can be processed both directly and in a logical sequence, a KSDS organization would probably be used. The KSDS type of organization is based on the association of two components called the data and the index. It is this index that provides the KSDS dataset with the capability of being processed directly, in logical sequence, or with a combination of both.

Entry Sequence Dataset (ESDS)

The user may select an ESDS organization whenever the dataset is to be processed in a physical sequential manner. The dataset is created by writing one physical block after another. The dataset may be blocked, that is, contain more than one data record per physical record; or the dataset may be unblocked, that is, contain one data record per block. The term "block" is used to loosely describe a control interval, which will be discussed later in this chapter. Records can be of fixed or variable length. The user defines an ESDS dataset in the cluster definition by specifying NONINDEXED. A cluster definition is where the user defines the VSAM dataset using a utility program called Access Method Services (AMS). The program that is executed is called IDCAMS. The use of this parameter in the cluster definition instructs VSAM to define an ESDS dataset. An example of an ESDS definition is given in Figure 1.1. ESDS datasets are useful for accumulating data that does not come in any particular sequence. An example of this would be a data entry application where the records are collected in random order and later are collated into sequence for processing.

Relative Record Dataset (RRDS)

If the processing characteristics of the dataset translate into having to access the data directly, the user can consider using an

```
DEFINE CLUSTER —
        (NAME (ENTRY.SEQ) —
        VOLUMES (VOL001) —
        CYLINDERS (10 2) —
        RECORDSIZE (100 100) —
        NONINDEXED) —
        DATA —
        (NAME (ENTRY.SEQ.DATA) —
        CISZ (4096))
```

Figure 1.1. VSAM ESDS cluster definition.

RRDS organization. This organization is the fastest method in VSAM of obtaining a record directly from a dataset. As the name of the organization implies, the records in this type of dataset are located by providing their relative position from the beginning of the dataset. Thus the first record written is relative record one from the beginning of the dataset, the second record written is relative record two and so on until the end of the dataset. The user can retrieve the tenth record in the file by providing a value of 10 to VSAM. The best analogy would be to picture an RRDS dataset as the mail/messages cubicles at a hotel front desk. Each cubicle has a distinct location and identifier. If the user wants data from one of these cubicles, the user only has to identify the desired cubicle or slot. Note that the space is available even though the guest may have checked out. In other words, the number of spaces to be reserved for an RRDS dataset must be predefined and/or established.

The user can develop different algorithms in order to locate the record in the dataset. One of these methods can involve the use of the record's key divided by a prime number close to the highest value that can be recorded for a key. By using the remainder as a relative record number, the user could locate a record in the dataset. To define an RRDS dataset, the user must specify the parameter NUMBERED in the cluster definition. An example of an RRDS definition can be found in Figure 1.2. The

```
DEFINE CLUSTER —
        (NAME (RELATIVE.FILE) —
        CYLINDERS (10 2) —
        VOLUMES (VOL010) —
        RECORDSIZE (150 150) —
        NUMBERED) —
        DATA —
        (NAME (RELATIVE.FILE.DATA) —
        CISZ (4096))
```

Figure 1.2. VSAM RRDS cluster definition.

main uses of an RRDS organization can be applications that require fast access to records in order to reply quickly to a query. An example of this is an online application.

Key Sequence Dataset (KSDS)

Whenever the user needs to be able to access a dataset directly as well as in a logical sequence, a KSDS dataset is usually selected. The KSDS dataset organization is different from the two previous organizations in that a KSDS dataset contains two separate components. The first component is the actual data stored in the dataset. The second component is an index through which a KSDS dataset can access the data directly or in logical sequence. The KSDS organization also allows the data to be processed directly to a specified location and then be processed sequentially from that point. Since the actual processing requires the use of the index, a KSDS dataset takes longer to process sequentially than an ESDS dataset and it takes longer to locate a record directly than an RRDS dataset. A KSDS organization provides the user with the best combination of two different access techniques (direct and/or sequential) in one dataset definition. The user specifies a KSDS organization by specifying INDEXED in the cluster definition. Figure 1.3 gives an example of how to define a KSDS dataset.

```
DEFINE CLUSTER —
        (NAME (KEY.DATA.SET) —
        CYLINDERS (10 5) —
        VOLUMES (VOL020) —
        RECORDSIZE (350 350) —
        KEYS (5 0) —
        SPEED —
        INDEXED) —
        DATA —
        (NAME (KEY.DATA.SET.DATA) —
        CONTROLINTERVALSIZE (4096) —
        INDEX —
        (NAME (KEY.DATA.SET.INDEX))
```

Figure 1.3. VSAM KSDS cluster definition.

The KSDS organization is usually used when a user wants to be able to directly access a master dataset online during the day and to update the dataset sequentially in batch processing during the night.

Linear Dataset (LDS)

Linear datasets are a special type of VSAM dataset announced to take advantage of the large virtual storage availabe in MVS/XA. Data in Virtual (DIV) is the concept with which a user can map the linear dataset to a virtual storage. This concept works well for tabular types of datasets when some of the parts of the dataset are not required, and other parts are referenced at least once. Performance gains can be achieved when the referenced areas are used more than once. Transfers occur in 4K CI sizes, making the dataset ideal for paging operations. This dataset organization is the first announced support under MVS V3 (ESA) that uses the new concept of dataspaces. As this is an evolving technology at this point, LDS organizations are not reviewed in this book.

VSAM ORGANIZATION

In this section we define the different terms used in organizing a VSAM dataset. A KSDS dataset is used as a model for defining the different areas in the dataset. The reader is urged to review this section as many times as required.

Control Interval (CI)

The basic unit of transfer of data in a VSAM dataset is called a Control Interval, or CI for short. A CI is used to define the unit of transfer of data from main storage to the disk or from the disk to the main storage. The CI can vary in size from 512 bytes to 8K bytes in increments of 512 bytes, and then to 32K in increments of 2K bytes. (A "K" is used to represent 1024 bytes.) As can be seen, the CI is defined as a fixed size with a minimum size of 512 bytes and a maximum size of 32K bytes. The selected CI size is constant for the entire portion being defined (data or index). So, if a CI size of 4096 bytes is requested for the data in a cluster, all the CIs in the data will be 4096 bytes in length. This means that the CI size must be large enough to hold the largest logical record plus a minimum of VSAM information. The logical records in the CI can be of either fixed or variable length. An exception to this is a spanned record, which will be discussed later in this chapter. Records can be held in the CI in either a blocked or unblocked format. In the case of a KSDS dataset, the data CI size can be different from the index CI size. This is because each area is considered to be independent even though they are related.

The concept of CI is similar to the previous concept of block size, but with one significant difference. The physical record size selected by VSAM may be different from the CI size. Depending on the CI size chosen, VSAM may select a physical record that is a multiple of the CI size. This is done by VSAM in MVS because the largest physical record written is a 4K block (prior to DFP 2.1). In the newer versions of DFP, VSAM tries to make the physical record size equal to the CI size. The exceptions are when the physical record size yields poor track utilization. For example, a 12K CI size uses two 6K physical records because there is better track utilization with a 6K physical record (42K) than with a 12K physical record (36K) on a 3380 disk unit. Whenever a CI is read or written, several physical records may be read or written with one I/O request.

In DOS, the process is different because VSAM may write up to an 8K physical record, depending on the disk unit used. As a result, DOS and MVS can generate different physical record sizes for the same CI size. The user can specify the CI size by using the CONTROLINTERVALSIZE parameter in the cluster definition. If the user elects not to specify the CI size, VSAM selects it for the cluster. Figure 1.4 details a CI with the different areas that can be found within a CI. Each CI has three basic areas:

- Data Area — used to store user data.
- Free Space — used to add or expand records.
- VSAM Control — provides internal CI information.

Each of these areas is addressed separately in the following sections.

One important note regarding CIs is that control intervals can span tracks but cannot span Control Areas, or CAs, which will be covered later in this chapter.

Data Area

The data area of a CI is used to store the user information of the dataset. The records are stored from left to right in the CI. Records can be either of fixed or variable length. Unless spanned records are used, the CI size must be large enough to hold the largest logical record. For a KSDS file, data records are loaded in logical sequence into the data portion of the CI. For ESDS files,

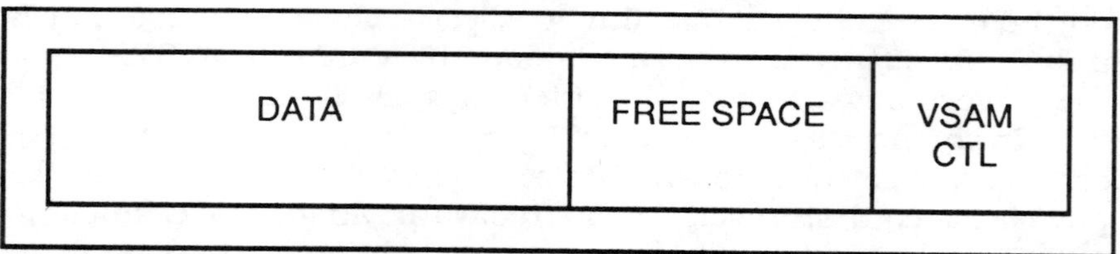

Figure 1.4. Control interval layout.

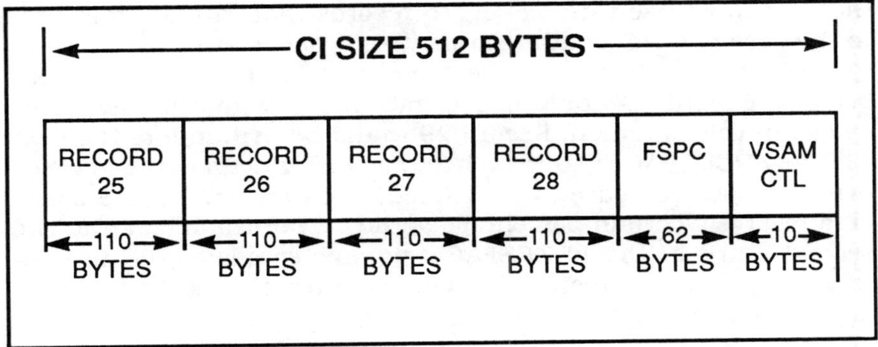

Figure 1.5. Data area layout.

the records are loaded in physical sequence. For RRDS files slots are written contiguously. Contrary to the Indexed Sequential Access Method (ISAM), CIs are not written in a Count-Key-Data (CKD) format. CIs are written in a Count-Data (CD) format. Data records are added to the CI as long as there is space to hold the record to be added. Additional considerations will be addressed when free space is discussed. Figure 1.5 illustrates how records with keys 25 to 28 are loaded into a KSDS CI.

FREE SPACE (FSPC)

Two types of free space can be found in a CI. The first results when the user asks for a particular percentage of the CI to be reserved for either the addition of future records or for the expansion of existing records as in the case of variable-length records. The user requests the percentage of free space desired by using the FREESPACE parameter whenever a cluster is defined. The use of this parameter results in an explicit way of obtaining free space.

The second way in which free space can occur is that the record sizes of the data were not a multiple of the CI size and VSAM control information. This free space is implicitly defined as a perfect fit is highly unlikely. This type of free space can be called "dead weight" in most cases. To use this type of free space the user must use variable-length records that can be expanded. In the case of fixed-length records, this space is lost.

Figure 1.5 illustrates the "dead weight" type of free space because Record 29 would not fit into this CI within the available space. In this situation, Record 29 would be written into the next CI. The FREESPACE parameter in the cluster definition allows for two types of free space to be defined. The first type of free space is to reserve a certain percentage of the CI, for example, 25%. The second entry in the FREESPACE parameter allows the user to reserve a certain percentage of control intervals within a control area to be completely free of data.

VSAM CONTROL INFORMATION

The VSAM Control Information is located at the end of every CI in the dataset. Since it is written at the end and in a particular format, VSAM knows how to locate it. The minimum size of this information is 7 bytes. The maximum length depends on the characteristics of the data being loaded. Figure 1.6 illustrates the format of the VSAM Control Information. A review of this figure will be helpful for the following discussion.

The control information consists of two types of fields, the Control Interval Definition Field (CIDF) and the Record Definition Field (RDF). The CIDF is always 4 bytes long and is used to con-

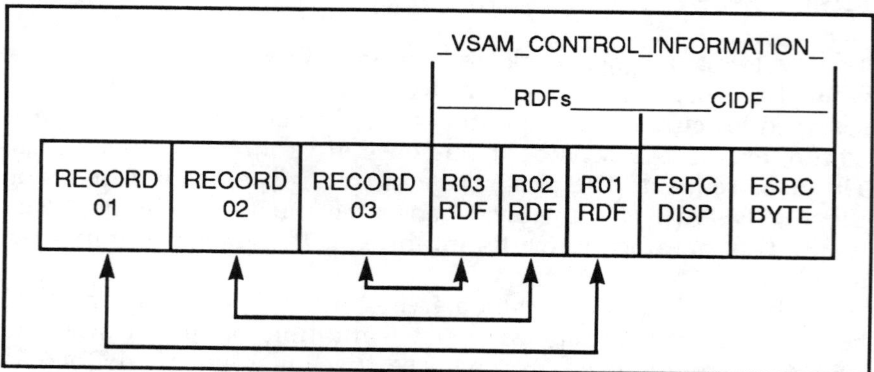

Figure 1.6. CIDF/RDF information layout.

trol the amount of free space left in the control interval. The CIDF is divided into two fields, each 2 bytes long. The first 2 bytes identify the displacement from the beginning of the CI to the beginning of the free space. The second 2 bytes identify the number of bytes in the free space. When a record is to be added or expanded, VSAM first checks the free space bytes in the CIDF against the total number of bytes requested. If space is available, the insertion is made. These two fields in the CIDF are maintained by VSAM.

Whenever a record is added or expanded, the pointer to the free space is updated by the requested number of bytes, whereas the total number of free space bytes is reduced by the number of requested bytes. Whenever a record is deleted or shortened, the opposite occurs. VSAM recovers space immediately and is available for use. The high-order bit of the CIDF free space length field (Byte 2) is turned on whenever a CI is being split. It is turned off when the split is completed. This is covered later in the chapter. There is only one CIDF per CI and it is always the last 4 bytes of the CI.

The second type of field available in the VSAM Control is the Record Definition Field (RDF). The RDF is 3 bytes long and is used to contain the record-length information. The RDF for each record in the CI is stored in the VSAM Control Area.

Note that the RDF fields are stored from right to left, whereas the corresponding data records are stored from left to right. Normally there is one RDF for each record in the CI. However, VSAM uses a coupling technique whenever two or more adjacent records are of the same length. In this manner, if the records in a CI are all of the same length, only two RDFs will be used to describe all the records in the CI. The layout of an RDF is given in Figure 1.7.

As can be seen from Figure 1.7, the first byte of the RDF contains a series of indicators whose use depends on the organization and situation being used. The two bits of interest at this point deal with Byte 0, Bits 1 and 4. VSAM has a special means of handling contiguous records of the same size. It is through the use of the mentioned bits (Byte 0, Bits 1 and 4) that VSAM is able to control the information in the RDF. First of all, let's examine the bits when record lengths vary between contiguous records. In

RDF BYTE	DESCRIPTION OF FIELD		
0	RDF Control Byte		
	Bit 0	—	Reserved (X'80')
	Bit 1	—	Blocked Record Information (X'40') If off = single record information If on = paired information (coupled)
	Bit 2–3	—	Spanned Record Indicator (X'10', X'20', X'30') X'00'—No X'01'—Yes, first segment X'10'—Yes, last segment X'11'—Yes, intermediate segment
	Bit 4	—	Next Field Contents Indicator (X'08') If off = Next 2 bytes have record length If on = Next 2 bytes contain the number of records
	Bit 5	—	RRDS Slot Indicator (X'04') If off = Slot contains a record If on = Slot is empty
	Bit 6-7	—	Reserved (X'03')
1-2	Binary Data depending on Byte 0 Bit 4 value:		If off = 2 bytes have the record length If on = 2 bytes contain the number of records

Note
This field is also used by spanned records to place the update number of the spanned record.

Figure 1.7. RDF information layout.

this case, VSAM would set Byte 0, Bit 1, to off, indicating that this RDF is only concerned with a single record. This means that this RDF corresponds to only one record. Since the RDF is used to indicate the record's size, then Byte 0, Bit 4, would also be off, indicating that the data contained in the next two bytes of the

RDF reflect a record length. This combination is the same for each individual record definition when the lengths vary.

However, the authors of VSAM realized that using this method for fixed-length records would result in an unusual amount of space going to control information. As a result, VSAM was designed to use two RDFs to define two or more contiguous records of the same length, thus saving space in the CI for data and not for overhead. For records of the same length, VSAM couples two RDFs to provide the necessary information. The first RDF is used to indicate the record's length and with the following RDF to provide the total information regarding the number of contiguous records. Byte 0, Bit 1, would then be set on while Byte 0, Bit 4, would be off in the first RDF. The second RDF would be used to indicate how many contiguous records there were. In the second RDF, Byte 0, Bit 1, would then be off, indicating that there were no more paired RDFs and Bit 4 would be on indicating that the next 2 bytes of the RDF contain the number of contiguous records. Note that the record length information is not carried in the record as with variable-length record formats available under other access methods. With the use of the RDF structure, VSAM can adapt to variable-length records quickly without having to restructure the data. We can say that VSAM is a variable-length system that accommodates fixed-length records. Figure 1.8 provides an example of the CIDF/RDF structure.

The smallest amount of VSAM control information that can be found in a CI is 7 bytes (one CIDF and one RDF) for unblocked records. Fixed blocked records require 10 bytes of control information (one CIDF and two RDFs).

The RDF also contains bits used by RRDS and spanned record support. Bit 5 is used by RRDS to indicate whether the slot contains a record (Bit 5 = OFF) or is empty (Bit 5 = ON). Bits 2 and 3 are used by spanned record support to indicate which segment (01 = first, 10 = last, 11 = middle) is contained in the CI. If both bits are off, there is no spanned record support.

Control Area (CA)

VSAM datasets are divided into a larger segment of information called a Control Area (CA). This area exists in all the organiza-

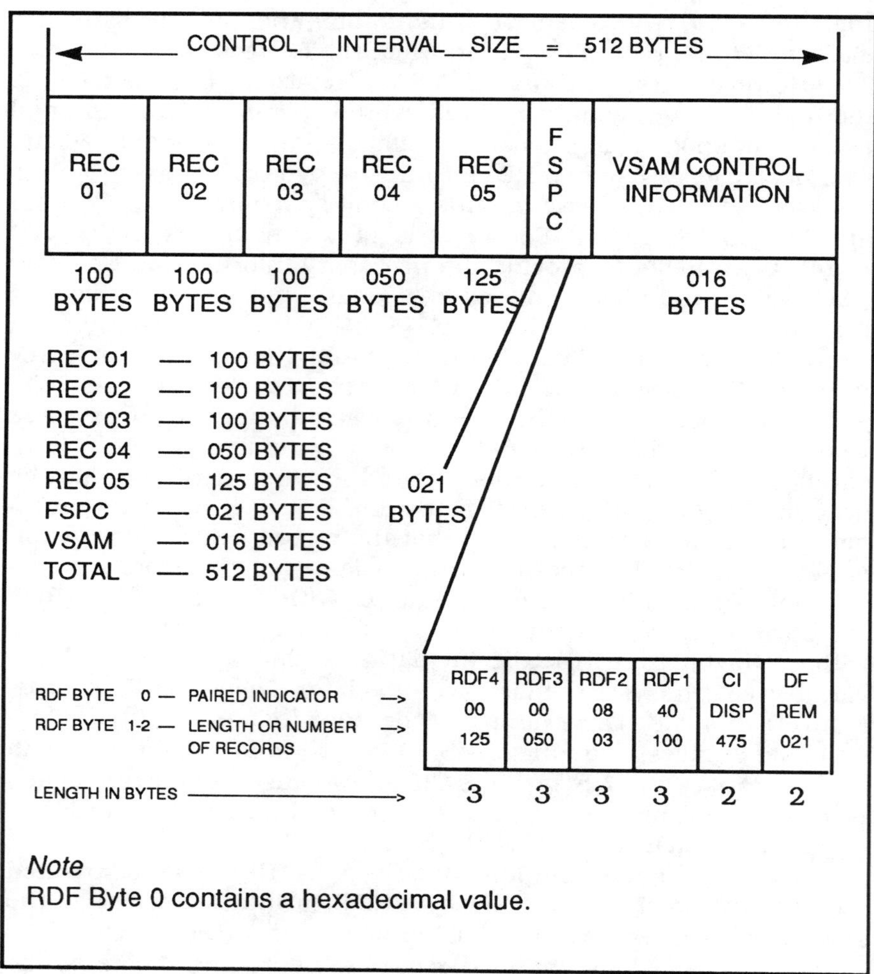

Figure 1.8. VSAM control information.

tions discussed. Depending on the organization used, the CA size can have some value in the tuning process. However, this is discussed in Chapter 5. Control Areas can be as small as one track for those using Count-Key-Data (CKD) disk units or 62 blocks for those using 3370 Fixed Block Architecture (FBA) disk units. One track or 62 FBA blocks is the smallest allocation that can be requested for a VSAM dataset. The smallest allocation is called a minimum CA. The maximum size that can be allocated to a CA is one cylinder for a CKD device or 744 blocks for a 3370 FBA device. For datasets that occupy a large space on disk, the objective would be to set the CA size to one cylinder, or 744 blocks. For smaller datasets, the objective would be to set the CA size to the maximum possible for the dataset size.

Once the CA size has been defined for a dataset, it remains constant for the entire dataset and can only be altered by reloading the dataset. The CA size is also constant across any expansions that may occur to the dataset. There are two components to a KSDS dataset: the data portion and the index portion. The data and index portions of a KSDS dataset can have different CA sizes since they are two separate but related entities.

No direct parameter is available to the user to set the CA size. This is different from the setting of the CI size, where a parameter exists in the cluster definition. The user indirectly selects the CA size. To select the appropriate CA size, VSAM uses the primary and secondary parameters in the dataset allocation as a guide. Space allocation can be requested in tracks, cylinders, or records for CKD disk units or in blocks or records for FBA disk units. The first rule that must be remembered is that all CA sizes within a logical area (index or data portion) must be the same.

VSAM selects the smaller of the primary or secondary allocation. In most cases, this is probably the secondary allocation although not necessarily. The selected unit is now compared to the minimum CA size, which is one CKD track, or 62 FBA blocks. If the selected amount is less than the minimum CA, the CA size is set to the minimum value of one track, or 62 blocks. A selection of less than the minimum CA size can occur when requesting space in RECORDS. If the user selected the space allocations in cylinders or multiples of 744 blocks, VSAM would set the CA to the maximum size, which would be one cylinder, or 744 FBA blocks. However, when the request is made in tracks or in FBA sizes that are not multiples of 744 blocks, the selection criteria that VSAM uses becomes somewhat complex. In these cases, VSAM could change the user's requested amount. This is because VSAM must have a CA size that is constant across the portion being defined. Therefore, VSAM makes sure that the CA size being defined is a multiple of both the primary and secondary allocations. As a result of this process, either the primary or secondary (or both) requested allocation could be altered either up or down. This is done to ensure the consistency of the CA size across the dataset. Figure 1.9 gives examples for CDK devices under DOS and MVS (ICF catalog).

The process for FBA units is similar. The selection of space in RECORDS can yield different results. The user is advised to review a LISTCAT to see the results of a request made in RECORDS format. Using RECORDS may make it more difficult to obtain the optimum CA size for the dataset. Several iterations of the DELETE and DEFINE IDCAMS process may have to be performed when using the RECORDS option. Large space requests using tracks or blocks may also require several iterations when the primary and secondary allocations are not a multiple of the maximum CA size for the device used. The same situation may occur when requesting space for a dataset in tracks or blocks and the primary and secondary allocations are not multiples of the maximum CA size as in the case of a large dataset or multiples of each other or as in the case of a smaller dataset.

There is one area of difference between DOS and MVS in this process. It occurs when the CA size is going to be less than one cylinder and IMBED (discussed later) is specified for the dataset. MVS adds one additional track to the requested allocation, whereas DOS does not. The only area where both agree is when the CA size would have been one track. In this case, since the IMBED specification would require the first track of the CA for the sequence set index, both DOS and MVS add one additional track to accommodate the data. Also, where the space allocation is requested (at the data, index, or cluster level) can also affect how the space is reserved.

Relative Byte Address (RBA)

One of the major advantages of VSAM is that it provides a certain degree of hardware independence. This is accomplished by maintaining the physical location of a record independent of the CDK disk address (BBCCHHR) or block address. VSAM looks at the

	REQUESTED CLUSTER ALLOCATION	WHERE WAS THE REQUEST MADE?	WAS EMBED SPECIFIED?	OPERATING SYSTEM	ACTUAL CLUSTER ALLOCATION	CONTROL AREA SIZE (TRACKS)	COMMENTS
1.	TRACKS (100 3)	DATA	NO	MVS/XA ICF	TRACKS (102 3)	3	PRIMARY ADJUSTED (UP)
	TRACKS (100 3)	DATA	NO	DOS/VSE	TRACKS (103 3)	3	PRIMARY ADJUSTED (UP)
2.	TRACKS (100 3)	CLUSTER	YES	MVS/XA ICF	TRACKS (100 4)	4	SECONDARY ADJUSTED (UP)
	TRACKS (100 3)	CLUSTER	YES	DOS/VSE	TRACKS (99 3)	3	PRIMARY ADJUSTED (DOWN)
3.	TRACKS (100 3)	CLUSTER	NO	MVS/XA ICF	TRACKS (99 3)	3	PRIMARY ADJUSTED (DOWN)
	TRACKS (100 3)	CLUSTER	NO	DOS/VSE	TRACKS (99 3)	3	PRIMARY ADJUSTED (DOWN)
4.	TRACKS (1 1)	CLUSTER	YES	MVS/XA ICF	TRACKS (2 2)	2	PRIMARY/SECONDARY ADJUSTED (UP)
	TRACKS (1 1)	CLUSTER	YES	DOS/VSE	TRACKS (2 2)	2	PRIMARY/SECONDARY ADJUSTED (UP)
5.	TRACKS (2 2)	CLUSTER	YES	MVS/XA ICF	TRACKS (3 3)	3	PRIMARY/SECONDARY ADJUSTED (UP)
	TRACKS (2 2)	CLUSTER	YES	DOS/VSE	TRACKS (2 2)	2	NO CHANGE
6.	TRACKS (3)	CLUSTER	NO	MVS/XA ICF	TRACKS (6 3)	3	PRIMARY ADJUSTED (UP)
	TRACKS (5 3)	CLUSTER	NO	DOS/VSE	TRACKS (6 3)	3	PRIMARY ADJUSTED (UP)
7.	TRACKS (5 3)	CLUSTER	YES	MVS/XA ICF	TRACKS (4 4)	4	PRIMARY/SECONDARY ADJUSTED (DOWN/UP)
	TRACKS (5 3)	CLUSTER	YES	DOS/VSE	TRACKS (6 3)	3	PRIMARY ADJUSTED (UP)
8.	TRACKS (100 3)	DATA	YES	MVS/XA ICF	TRACKS (100 4)	4	SECONDARY ADJUSTED (UP)
	TRACKS (100 3)	DATA	YES	DOS/VSE	TRACKS (102 3)	3	PRIMARY ADJUSTED (UP)
9.	TRACKS (97 3)	DATA	NO	MVS/XA ICF	TRACKS (98 7)	7	PRIMARY ADJUSTED (UP)
	TRACKS (97 7)	DATA	NO	DOS/VSE	TRACKS (88 7)	7	PRIMARY ADJUSTED (UP)
10.	TRACKS (97 7)	DATA	YES	MVS/XA ICF	TRACKS (104 8)	8	PRIMARY (SECONDARY ADJUSTED (UP/UP)
	TRACKS (97 7)	DATA	YES	DOS/VSE	TRACKS (98 7)	7	PRIMARY ADJUSTED (UP)

Figure 1.9. Sample CA size calculations.

data as if it were one continuous string of information or as a virtual storage address space. The records are stored in this virtual space one after another. Think of a dataset as being read completely into an unlimited storage area (e.g., a dataspace in ESA). The first record would be located at position zero (0) of this storage area. If the first record is 100 bytes long, the second record would be stored at location 100. If the second record is 350 bytes long, the third record would be stored at location 450. This is one of the concepts VSAM uses to provide hardware independence. The relative location of a record in the dataset is called its Relative Byte Address, or RBA. Through these means, the user need not care if CKD or FBA disk units are used because a records relative location would be the same on either device if other definition characteristics remain the same. Figure 1.10 further illustrates the concept of the RBA.

The RBA of a record cannot be changed in some of the VSAM organizations. ESDS datasets are accessed by RBA, although most of the time the user lets the access method handle the addressing method used.

REC 01	REC 02	REC 03	REC 04	REC 05	REC 06	REC 07	ETC.

RECORD NUMBER	LENGTH	RBA
01	100	0
02	125	100
03	100	225
04	125	325
05	100	450
06	100	550
07	100	650

Figure 1.10. Relative byte address (RBA).

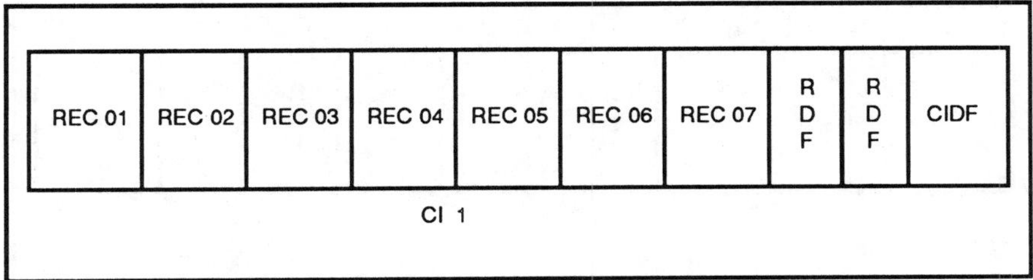

Figure 1.11. Fixed-length blocked record format.

RECORD FORMATS

VSAM supports most record formats supported by other access methods, although some may not be accessible from all programming languages. Support is available for both blocked and unblocked formats. The record format types available through VSAM are:

- Fixed-length records — where each of the logical records in the dataset are of the same length. This organization provides the lowest amount of VSAM control information in the CI because the minimum would be 7 bytes for unblocked records and 10 bytes for blocked records. A sample of this organization is given in Figure 1.11. RRDS datasets are an exception. RRDS records are of fixed length but require one RDF per record because there is a bit in each RDF indicating whether or not there are data in the slot.
- Variable-length records — where each logical record in the dataset can have a different length. This organization uses a variable length of VSAM control information in the CI because each record can generate an RDF. The minimum length for this control information can vary from a minimum of 7 bytes for unblocked formats to a number equal to an RDF per record in the CI, plus one CIDF. Whenever two or more records of the same size exist contiguously, VSAM takes advantage by using only two RDFs for their length control. A sample of this organization is given in Figure 1.12.

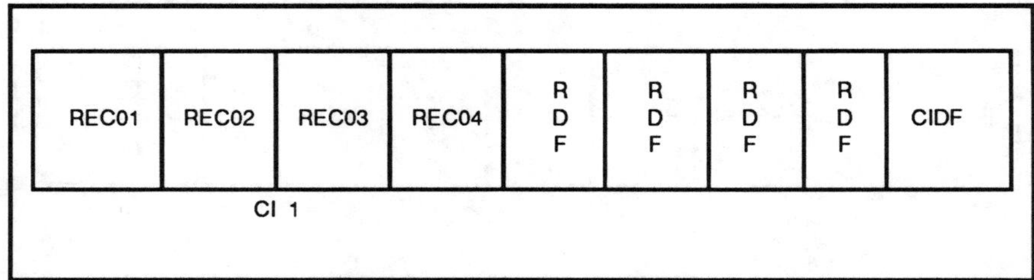

Figure 1.12. Variable-length blocked record format.

- Spanned-length records — a variable-length organization where the records may exceed the size of one or more CIs. This organzation is used for very large records. The control information is maintained in each CI for each part of the "spanned" record. A record that "spans" three CIs has 10 bytes of control information in each CI. Spanned records must begin on a CI boundary; therefore, any unused space in the last CI used by a spanned record is only available for use by the same spanned record. The next spanned record must begin in the next full CI. If the spanned record is going to be used in a KSDS organization, the record key must be located in the first CI of the record. A sample of this organization is given in Figure 1.13.

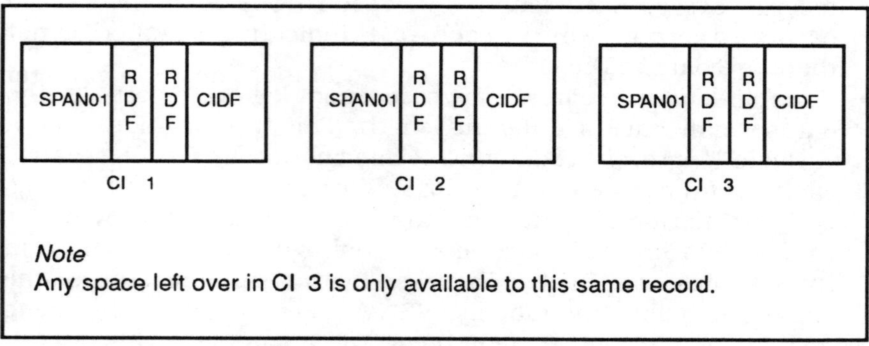

Figure 1.13. Spanned-length record format.

If a spanned record layout is to be used in the cluster, it must be defined in the original cluster definition prior to loading the dataset. VSAM is a natural variable-length record dataset and can accommodate fixed- or variable-length records in the dataset. This means that VSAM does not differentiate between fixed or variable records as long as the length doesn't exceed the maximum length specified.

KSDS Primary Index Structure

A KSDS dataset consists of two elements, the data portion, and the index portion. This is the basic difference between a KSDS and the other two organizations (ESDS and RRDS). The index component associated with the KSDS dataset is known as the Primary Index. The data and the index component can reside on different DASD units, which may be of different types. However, each component must reside entirely on the same type of device. The format used for the index portion is similar to the one used in the data portion. We review this layout in Chapter 2. The main purpose of the index is to provide a quick reference, which can be used to locate a record in the data portion.

The index contains the high key values of the data. To conserve space and make the index more efficient, these high key values are compressed. Compression occurs from the front of the key as well as from the back. The algorithm used is quite effective and in some cases can regenerate the key from a complete compression. Key compression is discussed in more detail in Chapter 2. Several levels of index layers are available. The lowest level of index is called the Sequence Set. All other levels are collectively called the Index Set. There is one sequence set index record per Control Area (CA). Each sequence set index CI contains a compressed key of the highest key of each CI in the data CA. If the data CA is composed of 60 CIs, the sequence set index CI will contain 60 data high keys, one per data CI. If a KSDS dataset has a total of 100 CAs, there will be 100 sequence set records, one per CA in the dataset. Remember that each sequence set record contains the high key value of each CI within a CA.

VSAM automatically builds a higher index level whenever one level expands and has more than one record. A second level (first level of the index set) is automatically created when the second sequence set record is built. VSAM always requires one index record to be the "boss" over the other levels. This organization is like a pyramid structure where there is always a single top. The new index record contains the high key value of each index record it controls. When this index set record gets full, VSAM automatically creates another record at the same level and since a "boss" is required because there is more than one index record at this level, VSAM automatically creates a new higher level. Most datasets have three or less index levels. Four levels requires a large dataset with a possible poor definition of the control area size. Figure 1.14 provides an example of a KSDS dataset.

The index and the data components may have different CI sizes as well as different space allocations. Certain parameters used in the cluster definition do not apply to the index portion. Note that the CI size for the index portion is one of the areas of incompatibility of datasets created in a DOS/VSE (VSE/SP) environment with OS (MVS/SP or MVS/XA). There are only four valid sizes for indices in MVS (prior to DFP 2.2): 512, 1024, 2048, and 4096 bytes. DOS (VSE/SP) creates other intermediate sizes as well as sizes greater than 4K up to 8K.

VSAM uses these indices to locate a record directly. VSAM searches for the appropriate index record by starting at the highest level index record. Each index record contains a vertical pointer to the next lower level index record. This chain is followed until the lowest level index record called a sequence set index is found. The sequence set index contains a pointer to the "candidate" data CI that should contain the desired data record. The use of the word "candidate" was intentional because it is not until the data CI is read that we can determine if the record for which we are searching actually exists.

There is no way to predetermine if a record exists because available data at the index levels consists of compressed high key values. For sequential processing, the index levels are followed until the lowest sequence set record is located; from there processing is accomplished by following a horizontal pointer that chains all sequence set records in order. The example in Figure 1.14 points out several important facts about the index structure of a KSDS dataset. First, the index CI size can and will probably be different from the data CI size. Next, a horizontal pointer is available for all index records. This horizontal pointer is used by index records of the same level to point to the next index record of the same level. Even though we can pictorially demonstrate the hierarchy involved in the index structure, the index records are all written out into one area sequentially unless the IMBED and/or REPLICATE options are selected. The index is flat sequential dataset. This horizontal pointer allows VSAM to find the next index record of the level being processed.

Another interesting point is that the keys in the index record are written right to left, with the lowest key occupying the high end of the index CI. This makes it easier to accommodate shifts in the key structure as new keys are added. One area not yet covered is the reservation of free space both within the CI and leaving completely empty CIs within the CA. This is covered in a later topic as it relates to a KSDS dataset. To access the dataset directly by key, VSAM begins its search for the key at the highest index level and works its way down until it locates the sequence set record that points to the candidate CI. To process the dataset sequentially, VSAM uses the same technique to locate the sequence set record with which to start processing. After processing the first CA, VSAM locates the next CA to be processed by following the horizontal pointer in each sequence set record. This pointer is used to logically maintain the CAs in logical order, which is not necessarily their physical order. The address (RBA) of the highest level index is maintained in the cluster definition in the catalog. Catalogs are discussed later in this chapter.

KSDS Free Space

The KSDS organization enables the user to add and delete records in the dataset. A user can also alter the length of the record in the dataset by either increasing or shortening it. This capability means that the record's RBA can be changed.

If a user is going to be extending a record length or adding records to a dataset, it would probably be prudent to specify some type of free space for the dataset. Two types of free space selection are available to the user. The user may first select free space at the CI level. This is done by specifying a percentage when defining the cluster or by an ALTER command after definition. This percentage is computed against the data CI size to determine how many bytes of the CI will be reserved for future expansion requirements. The other option available to the user is to reserve a certain percentage of completely free CIs out of the total in the CA. When the dataset is loaded, the CIs reserved for future expansion are not used. The effects of free space specification are covered in Chapter 3. For now, let us look at the merits of free space from the point of view that it is helpful for additions or for record length extensions.

In Figure 1.14, each of the defined CIs had a free space allocation of 20% at the CI level. It also had a free space allocation of 20% at the CA level. This allows us to accept at least one more record per data control interval. CI free space does not apply to those CIs reserved as completely free through the CA free space parameter. If a record within a CI is deleted, the space is automatically recovered and is available for immediate use. Control of the free space available in a CI is in the CIDF at the end of each CI. Control of completely free CIs is in the sequence set record. These areas are used whenever records are either added to the dataset or when a record is expanded within the same CI.

Control Interval/Control Area Splits

What happens when a record length needs to be expanded or a new record added, and there is no space available? VSAM handles this condition by doing a split. There are two types of splits:

- *Control Interval Split* — this type of split occurs when no more space is available within a control interval and more space is required for an addition or length extension. Although theoretically possible, a split can occur by reducing the length of a record by a very small amount in a completely full CI, which can cause the system to generate additional RDFs, requiring additional space in the control interval. This is a special situation. The vast majority of the splits are caused by the previous reasons of additions and record length extensions. The action the system takes depends on which way we were accessing the dataset (e.g., directly or sequentially) and where the insertion was going to be made in the CI. We review this in Chapter 4.

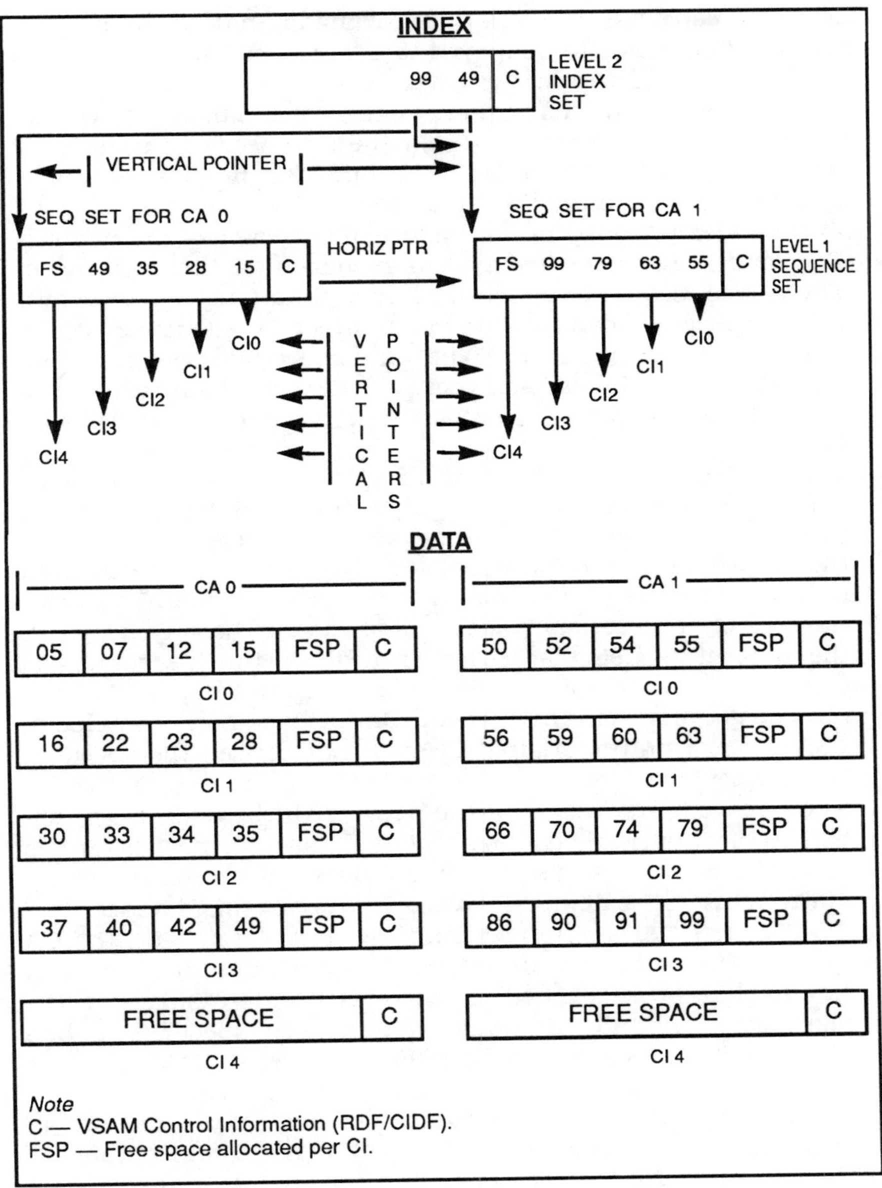

Figure 1.14. KSDS index/data layout.

For now, let us assume that approximately half of the records in the CI are going to be moved to a free CI. VSAM first tries to locate a free CI within the same control area. If a free CI is found by searching the sequence set record, half of the records are moved to the new CI. VSAM then proceeds to update its pointers in the sequence set to account for the fact that there is a new data CI in the CA. This involves the sorting of the keys in the index CI to maintain the logical sequence of the dataset. The data is not kept in physical sequence on the disk space. The correct sequence is provided by maintaining the keys with their associated control interval number in sequence in the sequence set index record. What happens when we need to do a control interval split, and there are no free CIs in the control area? Then we have the second type of split—a control area split.

- *Control Area Split* — this type of split occurs whenever a CI split is performed and a free CI is not available in the CA. VSAM then searches for a completely empty CA at the end of the dataset and uses that for the control area split. VSAM then proceeds to move part of the CA to this new location. The exact number of records, once again, depends on the way in which the dataset is being accessed and where the insertion was going to be made. As earlier, let us assume that half of the records get moved to the new CA. Once this move is completed, VSAM performs the original CI split that caused the CA split. What happens if no space is available at the end of the file when space is requested for the new CA? If the user has specified a secondary allocation for the dataset, a new extent is obtained as long as this new extent does not exceed the maximum number of extents allowed by VSAM for this dataset.

The new CA is obtained from this new extent and the CA split continues as just described. If the maximum number of extents has been reached, or there is no more space on the disk drive and no additional volume was specified, a bad return code is returned to the user. A nonzero VSAM return is usually handled by the user by canceling the program.

After the CA split, the dataset is now physically out of sequence. VSAM must now change the horizontal pointer of the CA split originator to point to the last CA in the dataset instead of the next CA. The horizontal pointer of the new CA is changed to point to the one to which the original CA causing the split was pointing. This chain now maintains a logical sequence.

Index Control

A method has to be established in order for VSAM to be able to handle the horizontal and vertical pointers. The method VSAM uses is quite simple. As mentioned previously, the CI size of each component in the dataset must be consistent across the entire component. If the data CI size is set to 4K, every CI in the data component is 4K in size. If the index CI size selected is 1K, every index record, whether a sequence set record or index set record, is 1K in size. This then makes it easy to talk about the relative CI record position. When you take the record's relative position within a CA and multiply it by the CI size, you have the record's Relative Byte Address (RBA) within the CA. Since everything is of fixed length, it is easy to convert the address to a physical DASD address (CCHHR or FBA block), depending on the type of drive on which the component is located. The same holds true for a control area. Control areas are constant in size for each component no matter where they are located on the DASD units or on which extent the desired information is located.

Associated with each compressed key in the sequence set index is the relative CI position in the CA to which this high key belongs. Also, within the index record is the RBA of the CA, which is associated with this index record. All that has to be done is to multiply the relative CI number by the CI size and add that total to the starting RBA of the CA to locate the RBA of the desired CI. This address can then be translated into the correct DASD address. We will see an index record layout in Chapter 2. When a CI split occurs, all that must be done is to take the new high key of the new CI and the relative CI number associated with this new key and place it into collating sequence within the sequence set record. When this key is processed, it will point to the correct logical CI to be processed for the key for which the search is being done.

Horizontal pointers are carried in RBA sequence from the beginning of the index component. Whenever there is a control area split, this pointer is updated to point to the RBA of the new index record. The new index record is written with the previous horizontal pointer held by the originator of the split in order to complete the chain. Even though most books depict the VSAM index as hierarchical, the index in reality is written as a straight physical sequential or special ESDS dataset.

Catalogs

Catalogs are available to locate and control VSAM datasets. Two types of catalogs are available to the MVS user to handle VSAM datasets. The DOS user only has one type of catalog available.

A VSAM catalog is available to the DOS and MVS user to catalog information regarding the dataset. The MVS user has another option called the Integrated Catalog Facility (ICF). In either case, the user must designate a catalog that will become the Master Catalog, which must be available when the operating system is IPLed. Due to its critical importance to the system, the master catalog should not be used for storing information about datasets. Instead, it is used to point to other catalogs called User Catalogs. More than one user catalog can be active in the system, but only one master catalog can be active in the system.

For the MVS user, ICF catalogs are more efficient than VSAM catalogs. In particular, the ICF catalog permits a volume to be owned by more than one catalog. This flexibility eases some of the previous constraints. Exclusive volume ownership is a restriction of VSAM catalogs. Another advantage of ICF catalogs is that VSAM space does not have to be allocated via the DEFINE SPACE IDCAMS command. All datasets are allocated using the MVS DADSM facility. Although the datasets appear to be UNIQUE in the IDCAMS LISTCAT listings, a dataset can still have up to 123 extents. VSAM and ICF catalogs are used for VSAM and non-VSAM datasets and should not be confused with the older CVOL catalogs available in OS. CVOL catalogs do not support VSAM datasets.

For the DOS user, VSAM catalogs are the only ones available. However, unlike MVS, a DASD volume may be owned by several VSAM catalogs in the newer versions of VSAM. Also, unless the user has the Sequential Access Method (SAM Extension) feature installed, DOS VSAM catalogs can only con-

STRUCTURE OR FACILITY	KSDS	ESDS	RRDS
Record Layout	Fixed Variable Spanned	Fixed Variable Spanned	Fixed Spanned
Access			
Sequential	Yes	Yes	Yes
Direct	Yes	Yes	Yes
Access By			
Key	Yes	Yes(1)	No
RBA	Yes	Yes	No
RRN (4)	No	No	Yes
Sequence	Logical Key	Physical Record	RRN(4)
Alternate Index	Yes	Yes	No
Features			
Deletion of Record	Yes	No	Yes(2)
Reuse of Deleted Space	Yes	No	Yes(3)
Change Record RBA	Yes	No	No
Addition of New Record	Anywhere	At EOF	Empty Slot
Change Record Length	Yes	No	No

Notes

1. Through Alternate Index.
2. Delete removes record, but slot remains.
3. If slot is empty.
4. Relative Record Number.

Figure 1.15. VSAM organization comparison.

tain VSAM-oriented datasets. Without this feature, the user must obtain third-party software to have "catalog" facilites for non-VSAM datasets.

As mentioned previously, the IDCAMS LISTCAT facility can be used to list the catalog information. This facility can be used to list information about the catalog and associated volumes. Individual dataset information can also be requested as well as the entire catalog. Anyone involved in the tuning process should be familiar with the information provided by a LISTCAT. Appendix A provides information regarding the important fields in a LISTCAT listing.

SUMMARY

The previous information is provided as a review. We believe that in order to tune VSAM, some knowledge about how it works and its organization is required. The previous data was only basic material to assist you in your tuning endeavors. If you want more information, we suggest that you read one of the two primer manuals referenced in Appendix C. Figure 1.15 summarizes the different VSAM organizations.

Chapter 2
CONTROL INTERVAL SIZE

This chapter reviews the data and index Control Interval Size (CISZ) and its effect on performance. The concepts presented in this chapter will assist the user in the selection of the Control Interval size. Many factors that affect this process are reviewed.

INTRODUCTION TO VSAM TUNING

Tuning is a continuous process. On too many occasions this principle is forgotten, especially in a growth environment. In many cases, tuning depends on other factors and resources. Tuning is a process where the user can trade a more abundant resource for a scarce resource. To do it well, the person performing the tuning process must have established beforehand which are the abundant and scarce resources. If plenty of resources are available, the user must project which ones have a likelihood of being scarce in the future. Users who do not have abundant resources do not have many choices. Resources that are usually of concern are:

- DASD space
- Virtual/real memory in the CPU
- CPU horsepower
- High channel and/or I/O device utilization
- A critical "processing window"

The preceding list is not all inclusive. There are probably many other resources. The important thing is to determine why the VSAM dataset must be tuned. Once this is done, the tuning process will be easier. You should evaluate the concepts presented in this book within your own environment.

Control Interval Size (Data)

Probably one of the most important areas of tuning a VSAM dataset lies in the tuning of the control interval size. In this chapter the effect of a good CI size is addressed for both the data portion and the index portion. In addition, we review the effect that the CI size has on the DASD physical record size. A control interval represents the unit of transfer that VSAM will use when reading data from disk into main storage or writing data from main storage to disk. This is similar to the concept used in other access methods, which referred to a block size. The difference in the two concepts lies in the way that VSAM formats the control interval. Depending on the CI size selected and the DASD unit used, VSAM may opt to write more than one physical record per CI. The selection varies by operating system, and the effect is different on each. For example, the largest physical block written by MVS is a 4K block when using an older DFP version.

Therefore, larger control interval sizes will be restructured into multiple physical record sizes of the requested physical record size. The I/O operation is accomplished by chaining the necessary Channel Command Words (CCWs). Several CI sizes result in a poor track utilization even though VSAM may try to correct the selection. Poor track utilization has two negative effects on performance. First, more DASD space is required to accommodate the dataset, thus wasting disk space. Second, the dataset takes more space, requiring more I/O operations to process, which in turn increases elapsed and CPU times as well as disk and channel contention.

The factors that affect the correct selection of the CI size are:

- The amount of DASD utilization expected. Is it a constraint?
- The type of processing that is going to be done on the dataset. Is direct or sequential (or both) processing going to be used?

- The amount of real and/or virtual storage available. Is either a constraint?
- Is a "critical window" associated with this dataset?

The effect of a poor CI size varies by DASD unit and whether the device is Count-Key-Data (CKD) supported by all operating systems or Fixed Block Architecture (FBA) supported by DOS and VM.

On a CKD unit, a poor CI size can result in poor track or CA utilization. In the case of an FBA device, the effect is not felt until the end of the CA. FBA units (e.g., 3370) can be compared to CKD equivalents by assigning a value of 62 FBA blocks equal to one track and 744 FBA blocks equal to one cylinder. The 3370 unit is roughly equivalent to a 3375 in its characteristics. Fragmentation is not seen until the end of a CA because FBA blocks are 512 bytes long. Therefore, if a CA is 744 blocks long, the ideal CI size would be a number that yields the least lost blocks when an entire CA is considered. Suggested FBA sizes based on the operating system used are given in Figure 2.1. The CI size recommendation is based on the page size.

CI Size	DOS/VSE	VSE/SP	VM/370 (SP/HPO)
1.0K	NO	NO	NO
2.0K	YES(1)	NO	NO
4.0K	YES	YES	YES
6.0K	YES	YES(5)	YES(5)
8.0K	YES(3)	YES(2)	YES(4)
12.0K	YES(3)	YES(2)	YES(4)
15.5K	NO	NO	NO

Notes
1. If the system is under a virtual storage constraint.
2. If the system has sufficient real storage.
3. If the system has sufficient real and virtual storage.
4. If the system has sufficient real storage and the guest has enough virtual storage.
5. If the total VSAM buffer allocation can be set to a multiple of 4K.

Figure 2.1. Recommended FBA CI sizes.

Note that there are some trade-offs based on external resources. DOS/VSE has a 16MB virtual storage limitation, which tends to limit some of the larger CI sizes because of the amount of virtual storage that can be assigned for use. This is especially true if the dataset is used in an online environment such as CICS/VS. DOS/VSE uses a 2K page size. Both VSE/SP and VM/370 use a 4K page size. The increased amount of virtual storage acquired with VSE/SP (128MB) and VM due to the capability of running several DOS systems will probably require more real memory to run effectively, and therefore, an increased CI size may be possible as well as desirable.

As mentioned earlier, poor CI selection results in poor track or CA utilization on CKD devices. In addition, although you may gain in space utilization by having VSAM fragment the CI size into smaller physical blocks, you are actually increasing the total time to do the I/O because of the additional gaps and control information involved in accessing the CI. There is one important difference between the physical record size generated by DOS and that generated by MVS (prior to DFP 2.2). The largest physical record size that can generate MVS (prior to DFP 2.2) is 4K in size, whereas DOS can generate a record up to 8K in size. This is of significance when you consider the 3380 DASD. You can fit 10 records of 4K into one track of 3380 for a maximum utilization of 40K. In DOS, either a 6K or 7K record can be generated, providing a track utilization of 42K. Figure 2.2 has the recommended CKD CI sizes for most of the devices available under DOS. Figure 2.3 has the recommended CKD CI sizes for MVS.

Once again, the trade-off is the amount of real and/or virtual storage available to you. If you are in doubt, start by using a CI size that yields a physical record size of 4K. A 4K physical record size is better oriented toward the size of a page in virtual and/or real storage. This is not the only criteria that can be used to select the best CI size. Each element can be selected independently, but the decision should be based on the installation requirements and/or constraints.

	3330		3340		3350		3375		3380	
CI SIZE	PHYS REC	TRK UTIL	PHYS REC	TRK UTIL	PHYS REC	TRK UTIL	PHYS REC	TRK UTIL	PHYS REC	TRK UTIL
2.0K	2.0K	12.0K								
2.5K			2.5K	7.5K	2.5K	17.5K				
3.5K					3.5K	17.5K	3.5K	31.5K		
4.0K	4.0K	12.0K	4.0K	8.0K			4.0K	32.0K	4.0K	40.0K
4.5K					4.5K	18.0K	4.5K	31.5K		
6.0K	6.0K	12.0K			6.0K	18.0K			6.0K	42.0K
6.5K							6.5K	32.5K		
7.0K									7.0K	42.0K
8.0K			8.0K	8.0K			8.0K	32.0K		
12.0K	6.0K	12.0K			6.0K	18.0K				
18.0K					6.0K	18.0K				

Figure 2.2. Recommended CKD CI sizes (DOS).

	3330		3340		3350		3375		3380	
CI SIZE	PHYS REC	TRK UTIL	PHYS REC	TRK UTIL	PHYS REC	TRK UTIL	PHYS REC	TRK UTIL	PHYS REC	TRK UTIL
2.0K	2.0K	12.0K								
2.5K										
3.5K										
4.0K	4.0K	12.0K	4.0K	8.0K			4.0K	32.0K	4.0K	40.0K
4.5K					4.0K	16.0K				
6.0K	2.0K	12.0K							6.0K(1)	42.0K
6.5K										
7.0K										
8.0K			4.0K	8.0K			4.0K	32.0K	8.0K	40.0K
12.0K	4.0K	12.0K							6.0K(1)	42.0K
18.0K										
22.0K									22.0K(2)	44:0K

Notes

1. DFP 2.2 and above.
2. DFP 2.2 and above (sequential processing).

Figure 2.3. Recommended CKD CI sizes (MVS).

PROCESSING CHARACTERISTICS

An important consideration in determining the CI size involves the processing of the dataset. Two major areas of concern are:

- Is the dataset going to be accessed online and/or batch?
- Is the dataset going to be accessed sequentially, directly, or both?

In the last section, we discussed the selection of the CI size for obtaining the best DASD utilization. In this section, we are going to analyze the preceding questions and their relative importance to the CI size selection.

Sequential Processing (Batch)

Processing a dataset sequentially in batch is straight forward. As the dataset is being read in a predefined order, the access method can provide a certain amount of overlap with processing by either reading ahead, as in the case of an input dataset, or writing behind, as in the case of an output dataset.

It is a general rule that for sequential processing a large CI is best. But the CI size should not be so large that it causes an undue amount of paging. If this occurs, an unnecessary amount of extra I/O is generated; this overhead can affect your program as well as the overall system throughput.

If these batch datasets are going to be processed when there is little or no online activity, the CI size can be relatively large. A CI size in the 8K–12K (or larger) range would be adequate. This is based on the theory that it is the online program (e.g., CICS/VS or IMS/VS) that puts the greatest stress on real and virtual storage resources. Our own experience has shown this to be true in most DP installations studied. If the dataset must be processed while the online program(s) is(are) operational, a moderate size (e.g., 4K–8K) is recommended.

The objective is to reduce the amount of operating system interventions required to service the dataset. Every time the operating system is called to provide a service either through a Supervisor Call (SVC) or through an I/O interrupt, no one else in the system is serviced while the supervisor attends to the request.

SVC and I/O interrupt routines account for thousands of instructions being executed, increasing the operating system overhead. If there are any storage constraints, it is better to have a large CI size instead of having multiple areas. CPUs today are extremely fast. It is not unusual to see two SVCs (EXCP and Wait) issued for an I/O request followed by an I/O interrupt from the device that informs the system that the operation was completed. Shared disk units between CPU complexes may result in more operating system overhead and interventions caused by contention for the disk units. This interference is caused by one operating system not being aware of the other operating system(s) operation on the desired unit. The higher the contention, the higher the overhead. This contention is reduced in an MVS/XA environment through better hardware. In these cases, there could be many interventions by the operating system code due to the contention for the device between CPUs (non-XA). The more interventions, the higher the supervisor overhead. The actual number of interventions varies with the operating system being used and system activity. For example, XA operating environments can handle this type of condition externally in the hardware. In an XA system, the channel subsystem provides a certain amount of queueing for device busy conditions, thus relieving CPU intervention. The operation, however, is still delayed.

Consider a dataset that has 100,000 logical records with each record having a length of 500 bytes. If a CI size of 2K is selected, up to 4 logical records per CI can be accommodated, meaning that the dataset would have a total of 25,000 CIs. Had a CI size of 4K been selected, 8 logical records per CI could have been accommodated. This would have reduced the total number of CIs in the dataset to 12,500. The actual number of operating system interventions depends on the operating system being used and the amount of buffer space provided for the dataset. However, in systems that have some sort of constraint, the more CIs that you have to process, the higher the overhead, real CPU, and elapsed times. Buffer space is reviewed in Chapter 6.

From the preceding example we can conclude that if there are three operating system interventions per CI processed (EXCP/Wait SVCs and an I/O interrupt), then to process the first dataset, a total of 75,000 operating system interventions would be required. If the CI size is doubled, only 37,500 interventions would be required. This would improve overall system throughput as well as the processing of the dataset.

Sequential Processing (Online)

Usually there is little or no sequential processing of datasets online. However, VSAM provides a facility called the browse feature. A user can use this feature to access a VSAM dataset at a particular point and start to read sequentially through the dataset. Due to the large amount of resources that this operation requires, many installations limit the use of this feature in an online environment. If your installation permits the use of the browse feature, you will have to evaluate the effect that a large CI will have on your overall online system. The possible major constraints that might be affected in an online system where browses occur are:

- The amount of virtual storage required for processing.
- The amount of real storage required for processing.
- The amount of channel, DASD control, and disk unit resources required for processing.
- The number of strings and data buffers required for processing the dataset.

For online sequential processing, an intermediate CI size of 4K is recommended. This CI size is sufficiently large to be able to provide good performance for both online and batch sequential processing. In addition, this type of transaction should be limited in the number of concurrent users so as to not affect overall system performance. Chapter 9 reviews tuning VSAM under CICS/VS.

Direct Processing (General)

Most of the documentation available today regarding the suggested CI size for datasets to be processed directly recommends a small CI size for the dataset. This recommendation is based on two generalized principles:

1. A small CI size reduces potential lockouts from other concurrent requests since fewer resources are being held under exclusive control for updating.
2. A small CI size is faster to read and takes up less main storage resources.

The preceding points are guidelines that may be true for some datasets to be processed in a direct manner, but this does not uniformly apply to all datasets. The first premise deals with the capability of multiple users to access the same record or CI concurrently. This concern is usually applicable to an online environment where accesses for a particular record can occur from more than one terminal. In a batch environment, you normally do not have multiple requests for the same record unless the dataset is being updated by more than one program at a time. In a batch environment, this normally occurs when the dataset is being accessed by an online program while being updated from a batch program. It is the user's responsibility to ensure data integrity in this environment.

The second consideration regarding the first principle is the size of the dataset. A dataset that contains a large number of records reduces the probabilities of concurrent access. A small number of records increases the probabilities of a concurrent request. To illustrate the two points, consider a bank customer checking file that has 350,000 master records. What are the probabilities of two tellers wanting to access the same record or CI simultaneously? If it is an individual account (e.g., a personal checking account), the odds are very low. If the account is a company account, the probabilities would be higher but not significantly. However, consider that each time a transaction occurs, the teller and branch total records have to be updated. If there are 500 tellers and 50 branches, the probability of concurrent access increases significantly. In this last case, multiple accesses to exclusive resources can affect performance. An exclusive resource is one that can have only one owner at a time when an alteration of the record is possible. Subsequent requestors would have to wait until the current owner releases the exclusive use of the resource before being able to access the data.

An important aspect of the CI size with regards to resource consumption is the amount of virtual and real storage used for I/O buffers for the dataset. If the amount of real or virtual storage available is limited, a smaller CI size would be more prudent to reduce these constraints. This is particularly true if many datasets are involved

The second principle is an interesting one. (It has been part of the recommendations given to programmers and system designers since the mid-1960s.) To fully understand why this recommendation was made, we have to evaluate the type of DASD units available in those days. The main unit available when the S/360 was announced was a 2311 Disk Unit. This unit had a total capacity of 7.25MB with a transfer rate of 156KB per second. It had 200 cylinders. The drive had ten tracks per cylinder with each track having a capacity of 3625 bytes. Average access time was 75ms. Microcomputers today have access to much more powerful disk drives.

When accessing a record on a DASD unit, three major components make up the total time to access the record. There is a seek, which is the movement of the arm to the correct cylinder and track. This operation is followed by a search for the record, forgetting about Rotational Position Sensing (RPS),which involves waiting for the record to spin under the read/write head. Finally, there is the actual read or write when the record is under the head. If you consider RPS, additional time factors are involved such as RPS misses. For purposes of this analysis, RPS is not important, although it reduces channel contention and/or utilization, which are important factors making new DASD devices more efficient than older devices. Figure 2.4 gives you the timing and track utilization information for different block sizes on a 2311.

From Figure 2.4, chart, we can observe that the total read time required for a record versus the overall time grew significantly as the block size grew (3.6% versus 20.8%). Thus, as the block size grew, so did the overall time to read the block. The situation today is different. DASD units have more capacity and are much faster. In fact, the performance of these modern units is adversely affected by small block sizes. Figure 2.5 provides a similar comparison to an IBM 3380 unit.

Block Size	0.5 K	1.0 K	2.0 K	3.5 K
Average Seek	75.0 ms	75.0 ms	75.0 ms	75.0 ms
Average Rotational Delay	12.5 ms	12.5 ms	12.5 ms	12.5 ms
Average Read Time	3.3 ms	6.6 ms	13.1 ms	23.0 ms
Total Time	90.8 ms	94.1 ms	100.6 ms	110.5 ms
% of Read Time of Total	3.6 %	7.0 %	13.0 %	20.8 %
% of Track Utilization	84.7 %	84.7 %	56.4 %	98.9 %

Figure 2.4. 2311 timings and track utilization.

Block Size	0.5 K	1.0 K	2.0 K	4.0 K
Average Seek	15.0 ms	15.0 ms	15.0 ms	15.0 ms
Average Rotational Delay	8.3 ms	8.3 ms	8.3 ms	8.3 ms
Average Read Time	0.2 ms	0.3 ms	0.7 ms	1.4 ms
Total Time	23.5 ms	23.6 ms	24.0 ms	24.7 ms
% of Read Time of Total	0.9 %	1.3 %	2.9 %	5.7 %
% of Track Utilization	49.61 %	66.86 %	77.65 %	86.28 %

Figure 2.5. 3380 AD4 timings and track utilization.

As can be seen from Figure 2.5, the new high-capacity DASD units are adversely affected in their overall storage capacity by small block sizes. In addition, note that the total time to read the block is a very small proportion of the overall time to access the block. A similar comparison can be made for other modern DASD units. With the high transfer rates available on modern DASD units, the time required to read a large block versus a small block is not as significant as it was when the 2311 disk drive was in use. Two of the three elements, seek and search, are the same regardless of the block size. The third element does not represent any value significant enough to justify the use of a smaller block size.

Based on the preceding 3380 table (Figure 2.5), we can observe that the total time to read a larger CI size (0.5K versus 4.0K) is not sufficiently long that a person accessing the file online will notice the difference. To gain one second of time, the application would have to read approximately 833 records, as shown in Figure 2.6.

Time to read a 4.0K CI	1.4 ms
Time to read a 0.5K CI	0.2 ms
Difference	1.2 ms

1000 ms per second ÷ 1.2 ms per record = 833.3 records

Figure 2.6. Timing comparison.

One last area to be considered when determining the CI size for a dataset that is to be accessed directly, is the amount of time it takes to back up and restore the dataset. The smaller the CI size, the higher the amount of overhead because it will take longer to back up and restore the dataset. This can be an important consideration for those installations that load their online VSAM files every day before the offices or branches open for business.

These datasets are usually created immediately after the batch processing has completed the night's posting of transactions. There is a "critical window" associated with the time left between the ending of the batch runs that permit the loading of the dataset to the time when the datasets must be available for the users for everyday operations. The period when users need the data is normally in the early morning (8:00 or 9:00), as the offices open for business. This period is usually inflexible because you can't tell customers to go away and come back later when the files are loaded.

The end of the batch runs can usually be predicted under normal circumstances. However, outages due to program, hardware, or human error can significantly reduce the time available for this "critical window." In these cases, the load times are an important process in establishing the CI size. The larger CI sizes have better load times under equal circumstances. Using Figure 2.6 as a base, let's analyze the number of online reads that would be required to recover the time difference caused by using a smaller CI for a dataset. Suppose that the loading of a dataset using a 0.5K CI took 30 minutes more than when the dataset had a 4.0K CI size. Figure 2.7 demonstrates the number of online reads required to recover the difference in load times.

Difference to access a 4.0K CI	1.4 ms
Number of records to = one second	833 records
Load time difference in seconds	
(30 min. * 60 sec./min.)	1800 seconds

1800 seconds * 833 recs./sec. = 1,499,400 records

Figure 2.7. Load time breakeven analysis.

This is a significant number of records to access directly in order to recuperate the additional load time, especially if the dataset is created every day. If the dataset is not created daily, this figure must be factored to include the number of days that elapse before the dataset is reloaded. The daily back up time must be added into this computation.

The following general guidelines should be used in selecting the CI size for a dataset that is to be accessed directly:

1. For datasets with a possible small number of records and possible simultaneous requests being issued to the same record or CI, try to keep the CI size as small as possible to reduce or eliminate contention. Suggested size should be around 0.5K–2K for the CI. One logical record per CI is preferred.
2. For large datasets where the possibility of concurrent requests for the same CI are very low, use a larger CI size. Suggested size should be around 4K–8K for the CI.
3. For systems that have real and/or virtual storage constraints, use the largest possible CI size that will not worsen the situation. Suggested CI size should be around 2K–4K.
4. Newer versions of VSAM (e.g., DFP 2.2 and above) provide a better relationship between the CI size and the physical record size. As a result, better track utilization can be obtained. In particular, a 22.0KCI size will result in a 22.0K physical record size. This CI size is particularly good for datasets processed

strictly sequentially and provides the best VSAM track utilization on a 3380.

Direct Processing (Batch)

As mentioned in the previous section, the size of the CI will be affected by the activity and size of the dataset. The guidelines provided in the previous section are adequate for this type of processing.

One consideration when discussing very large direct files is the total DASD space required to accommodate the file. If the CI size is made to be very small, the file is going to occupy more space on the disk unit than if the CI size were made larger. This is of particular importance because the term "average seek" is used to represent the amount of time required by a disk unit to cover one-third of the cylinders on the unit. If the dataset is very large and requires more space than one-third of the DASD unit, the average access time could be longer than if the file had been compacted with a larger CI size. The actual total effect depends on the access pattern. For example, if we can prearrange the transactions so that the arm is continuously moving forward, the access motion could be reduced. The activity on the disk unit from other tasks also affects performance by stealing the arm and/or creating path busy situations.

In general terms, the direct batch processing of applications does not normally place any pressure on the system's virtual or real storage requirements during the processing of the dataset. Frequency of loads and the time required for these loads are considerations that should be used in determining the CI size. Time required for backups should also be considered.

Direct Processing (Online)

The major concerns when processing a direct file in an online environment are:

- The possible contention created when two or more tasks are trying to access the same record or CI requesting exclusive control.

- The amount of virtual and real storage that is required to process the record or CI.
- The length of time the record or CI is held if it is a protected resource (e.g., Dynamic Transaction Backout).
- The length of time that it takes to back up or restore the file for normal and emergency processing.

The preceding factors are important in the determination of the CI size for the dataset. The guidelines provided in the general section on direct processing are valid for datasets processed directly. The size of the dataset and the possibility of contention for resources are two important factors in determining the CI size for the dataset in an online environment. If the contention situation is not a problem, a CI size of around 4K can be considered adequate for most DASD units. The amount of GETVIS or OSCOR (for delayed open) required to process the dataset is also a consideration. They are discussed in Chapter 9. Many large online users are facing upgrades of their operating systems to MVS/XA or VSE/SP in order to provide relief from the amount of virtual storage required to process the datasets online. Chapter 9 addresses the CICS/VS considerations for VSAM dataset.

CI Size Selection When Using Small Logical Records

The creation of small, heavily accessed datasets presents an area for special consideration. Small, heavily accessed datasets are candidates for contention problems. A teller total file is an example of this type of dataset. Ideally, we would like to define one logical record per CI to reduce contention. However, the smallest CI that can be defined is 512 bytes long. If the logical record size were 100 bytes long, we would have five logical records per CI, an amount that may still be too high.

A possible solution to this situation is to redefine the record size from 100 bytes to 500 bytes by simply adding a 400-byte filler at the end of the record. Unfortunately, this solution would require the recompilation of all programs that access the dataset. This process may take some time, plus the exposures inherent to the recompilation process such as finding the correct version of the program. The amount of testing required due to Change Management controls may also be lengthy and expensive.

A better solution to this situation is to load the dataset requesting a free space allocation of 80% at the CI level. This would result in only one logical record per CI being loaded, the optimum in a high contention environment. This solution assumes that if new records are added to the file, a reorganization would take place before the dataset is made accessible to the contention environment. The advantage is that it can be implemented quite simply by reloading the dataset. Usually, small files, which are the candidates for contention problems, can be reloaded quickly.

Fragmentation and the CI Size

Fragmentation in a CI occurs whenever the sum of the logical record sizes does not fit exactly into the total space reserved in the CI minus the VSAM control information. This space can be used in the expansion of variable-length records. For fixed-length records, this area is lost. When deciding on the CI size, it may be worthwhile to review the total amount of fragmentation in the CI versus other CI sizes. This is especially true when the logical records are large and close to CI size multiples. For example, suppose that a logical record were 1020 bytes long. If the user selected a CI size of 2048, only record per CI would fit because two records would require 2040 bytes plus 10 bytes for VSAM control information. This would exceed the 2048 bytes by 2 bytes. The total loss would be 1017 bytes or 49.7%. A 1K CI would be too small because a minimum of 7 bytes would be required for VSAM information. An important note on the selection of the CI size is that if the user does not specifically request the CI size, VSAM could select a 0.2K CI size for the cluster regardless of the loss of space. A better selection would be a 4K CI, yielding a loss of only 6 bytes, or 0.1%. This would be an almost perfect fit, four records would fit in a 4K CI.

Consider one final note regarding the logical record size. Because VSAM CIs are in multiples of 512 bytes, logical record lengths that are close to this multiple could yield poor results. This is due to the loss to VSAM control information. For example, a logical record size of 256 bytes yields a loss of 246 bytes when fixed-blocked records are used. This is due to the 10 bytes of VSAM control information required for fixed-length records discussed in Chapter 1. If the logical record were reduced to 255 bytes, then, at a 4K CI, 16 records instead of 15 would fit in the CI. The loss would be only 6 bytes instead of 246.

CI Size for Very Small Datasets

Certain datasets do not justify a 4K (or larger) CI size. This occurs when the number of records in the dataset is small combined with a possible small logical record length. If the dataset is processed in a batch mode instead of accessed online, you should make the CI size large enough to cover the number of records times the logical record length. In some cases, this may result in making the CI size larger than 4K. However, the entire file can be read with one read operation.

If the dataset is accessed in an online environment, some additional considerations may have to be analyzed. If the dataset is accessed using Non-Shared Resources (NSR), the batch rules can be applied to the dataset as long as the CI size does not place a constraint on the real or virtual storage. If the dataset is assigned to a Local Shared Resource (LSR) pool, some consideration should be given to avoid making the data CI size the same size as index CIs. If this is done, the data CI size may compete with other index CIs for buffers. Buffers are allocated using the Least Recently Used (LRU) algorithm. Also, LSR buffer CI sizes do not cover all the CI combinations available to VSAM. For more information on CICS/VS, see Local Shared Resources (LSR) in Chapter 9.

Recommendations for the Data CI Size

The user should always specify the CI size for the data, otherwise, VSAM will select it. The default is not always the optimum size for the dataset. Always adapt the CI size to the environment of the dataset. The first area to be determined is the critical resource in the system. This critical resource can be virtual or real storage, DASD space, "critical window," or load times (back-up and restore). Consideration must be given to the operating environment, which includes DASD type, real memory available, operating system used, and type of processing, for example, direct or sequential in an online or batch environment.

When choosing among different CI options, select the one that yields the best blocking factor with the least amount of space lost to fragmentation. The size should be the one that yields the best track utilization for CKD units and least fragmentation at the end of a Control Area (CA). For FBA devices, the fragmentation occurs at the end of the Control Area.

For sequential processing, select a large CI size. A 4K–8K CI is adequate, although larger sizes can be selected. For direct processing, select a size that is not too small unless the dataset requires it to reduce contention. A CI size of 4K is generally acceptable if there is a low probability of contention. There is one final consideration in selecting the data CI size. Make sure that the size is specified at the data definition level and not at the cluster level, ensuring that the CI size selected applies only to the data portion of the file. If it is defined at the cluster level and this is a KSDS file, the definition will also apply to the index portion. This may turn out to be too large, creating unused space in the index record, which wastes virtual and real storage.

CONTROL INTERVAL SIZE (INDEX)

The index control interval size can be an important factor in the definition of a KSDS dataset. The index definition is a basic area of difference between the operating systems used (e.g., MVS or DOS). DOS (VSE and SP) can have an index that varies from 0.5K to 8K, whereas OS (MVS and VS1) varies from 0.5K to 4K in size. Also, DOS can have index sizes that are not available to OS. For example, OS only uses four index sizes, which are 0.5K, 1.0K, 2.0K, and 4.0K, whereas DOS uses these and other sizes such as 1.5K. The index CI size restrictions have been eased with the newer releases of DFP under MVS/XA. Index CI sizes can now be larger than 4K. This is an area that has to be controlled in those environments where dataset access between OS and DOS is desired.

Note, also, the inverse relationship between the index and data CI size when working with a large Control Area (Max-CA). Whenever the data CI size is made to be small, the index size will be large. The opposite is true: if the data CI size is made to be large, the index CI size can be smaller. An inverse relationship occurs because of the number of index keys that must be stored in the index record. Smaller data CIs create more CIs per CA, requiring a larger index CI size to hold additional keys.

Most of the time, it is better to let VSAM select the index CI size. The user may want to override the index CI size selected by VSAM in four cases:

1. When the dataset's key is unusually large and the key compression algorithm is partially successful. This has the effect of losing space within a Control Area (CA).
2. When the number of Control Areas (CA) in the file can be predicted and will remain relatively constant. This controls the number of index levels in the dataset.
3. When a Local Shared Resource (LSR) pool is used so that the index and data CI sizes are forced to be of different sizes so that they do not compete for the same buffer sizes.
4. For dataset access options between DOS and OS. The user may want to force a DOS index size that is compatible with OS.

All of these cases are discussed in the following sections.

Key Compression

VSAM uses a technique called key compression to reduce the number of bytes required for the index CI. This compression occurs both at the front of the key as well as in the rear of the key. Front key compression is easy to visualize since it involves the removal of duplicate information contained in the key. If you take a look at a credit card issued by a bank and compare the account number to a similar credit card from the same bank, you will note that the first few digits are the same. These digits usually refer to the bank and cycle numbers. Everyone who has a card issued from this bank will have identical starting digits. VSAM compares the beginning of one key to the beginning of the next key in the index and truncates the unneeded digits from the second key. The first key is the root key, which is used to generate the digits of the next key. The second key is now used to generate the third key and so on. Since the missing digits are contained in the previous keys, it is a simple routine to generate the missing high-order digits of any key following the base key. If the account number changes dramatically, like moving to another bank, then VSAM generates a new root and starts the process over again. This is also done for new index records.

Rear key compression is a little harder to visualize. The main idea is to remove insignificant information from the end of the key. This process involves the determination of what is the significant difference between the key being processed and the next key to be processed. When the significant position is determined, all subsequent digits are deleted or truncated.

Since VSAM does not carry the necessary information in the previous keys to generate the digits that were truncated, how does VSAM reconstruct the end of the key? The answer is really quite simple. VSAM regenerates the end of the key by filling out the missing bytes with X'FF' (HIGH-VALUES). This forces any key that has a lower value than the generated key to be placed in the current CI. Two important effects are caused by this technique. The first effect is that you could force a higher value key into a CI that was loaded with a lower key value. For those who have used ISAM, this is different. The original high key value in ISAM is respected with all new additions. The second effect created by this technique is that you could generate a key that contains no key information due to the front and rear key compression. This means that VSAM has to recreate the entire key from the control information provided.

The layout of an index CI follows the general rules of a VSAM CI layout. However, the structure of the information is completely different. A layout of an index CI can be seen in Figure 2.8.

The VSAM Control Information is 24 bytes long. It is contained in each CI found in the index structure. The information contained within this field is used to determine the following:

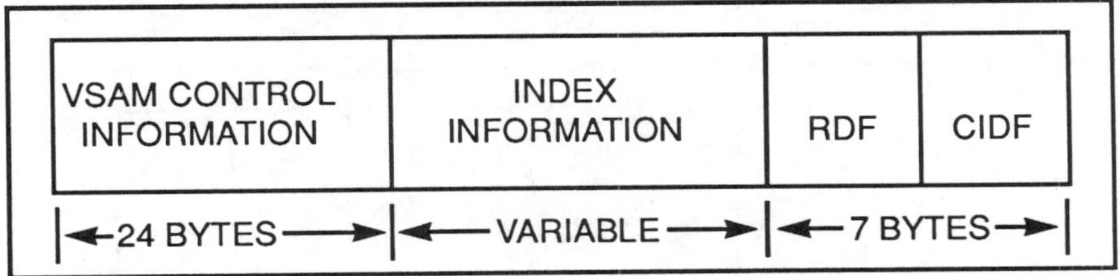

Figure 2.8. VSAM index CI layout.

- The length of the index record
- The length of the key control field
- The index level number
- The horizontal pointer
- The RBA of the CA
- The displacements to the high key and unused space

The index levels begin with X'01' for the sequence set and are incremented by one for each level. All horizontal pointers are in the format of an RBA from the beginning of the index file. The key control information indicates whether a 1–, 2–, or 3–byte pointer is being used to refer to the relative CI number within the data CA. The description of this area can be found in the VSAM logic manual.

The index information area is where the compressed keys are kept. VSAM stores the keys and associated control information starting with the lowest key at the end of this area next to the RDF/CIDF. The keys are stored from right to left or from the high end of the record to the low end, as was illustrated in Figure 1.14.

Associated with each key is a key control area, which can be 3, 4, or 5 bytes long, depending on the number of bytes needed to point to the relative CI number. The length is specified in the VSAM Control Information at the beginning of the index record. A layout of this area can be seen in Figure 2.9.

This area is also used to control whether there are any free control intervals within the control area. Using a pointer located in the VSAM Control Area at the beginning of this record, VSAM locates the next available CI number, if any. These CIs are used during CI split processing. If none is available, a CA split is in order.

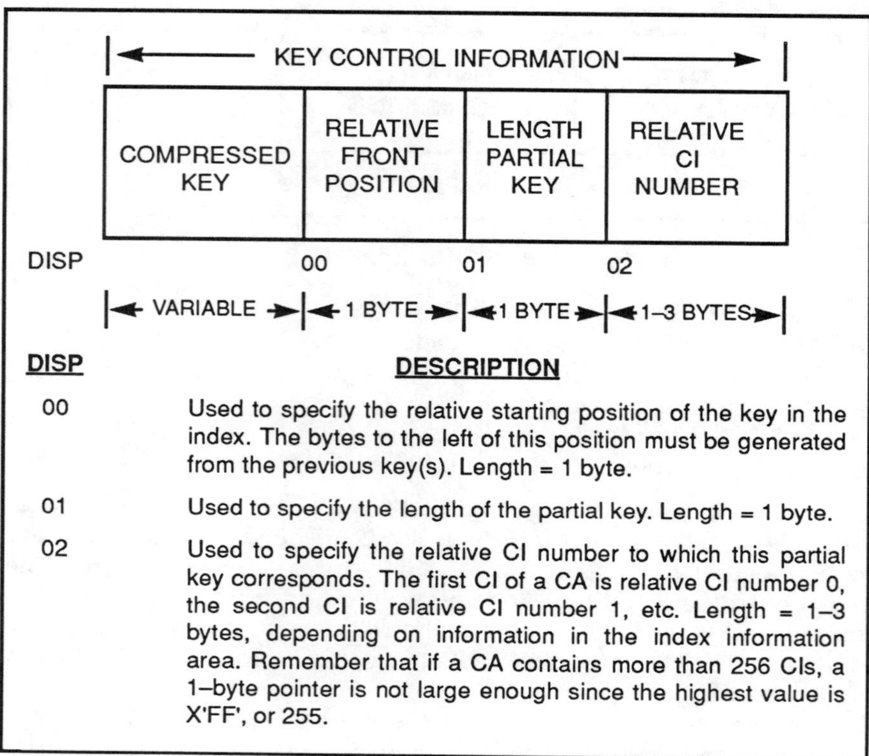

DISP	DESCRIPTION
00	Used to specify the relative starting position of the key in the index. The bytes to the left of this position must be generated from the previous key(s). Length = 1 byte.
01	Used to specify the length of the partial key. Length = 1 byte.
02	Used to specify the relative CI number to which this partial key corresponds. The first CI of a CA is relative CI number 0, the second CI is relative CI number 1, etc. Length = 1–3 bytes, depending on information in the index information area. Remember that if a CA contains more than 256 CIs, a 1–byte pointer is not large enough since the highest value is X'FF', or 255.

Figure 2.9. Layout of key control area.

VSAM uses the key control information to generate the appropriate key value that will point to the proper CI where the record should be located. VSAM does not know whether or not the record exists until the whole data CI is read into storage and each record is compared to the argument value. If a key is completely compressed, all that will exist is the key control information within the index area.

The final area of the index CI is the RDF/CIDF area. These fields work in the same fashion as in a regular CI. As there is only one RDF, the record is unblocked. VSAM manages the fields within the data area individually.

Problems With Key Compression

The algorithm that VSAM uses is usually efficient to reduce large keys into small partial keys. MVS VSAM does not directly use the length of the key to determine the CI size to be used. Instead, VSAM has a predetermined CI size based on the number of CIs per CA. Remember that VSAM has to keep the highest key value in each CI within a CA in the sequence set record. Figure 2.10 depicts the table that MVS VSAM uses to determine the index CI size.

NUMBER OF CIs/CA	INDEX CI SIZE
1 ≤ No < 58	.5K
58 < No < 120	1.0K
120 < No < 248	2.0K
248 < No < 502	4.0K

Figure 2.10. Index CI size (OS).

DOS has a similar table, but it includes intermediate and larger CI sizes. More recent versions of MVS DFP also use intermediate sizes like DOS and larger than 4K index sizes. VSAM permits you to make the CI size larger than the default but does not let you specify a smaller value. If a smaller value is specified in the cluster definition, VSAM automatically increases it to its default size. VSAM does not issue a message that this has been done. This also happens with the data CI size specification when you define a record size greater than the CI size without specifying SPANNED support.

Suppose that you define a cluster that has 55 CIs/CA and a key length of 12 bytes. VSAM is going to use an index CI size of 512 bytes. Figure 2.11 tries to demonstrate how well the VSAM compression algorithm must work in order to fit all of the 55 required keys into a 512-byte CI.

Index CI Size	512 bytes
minus VSAM Control Information	– 24 bytes
minus RDF/CIDF	– 7 bytes
Total Bytes Left for Keys	481 bytes
Number of CIs/CA	55
Average Compressed Key Size	8.75 bytes (481 bytes/55 CIs)
minus Key Control Information	– 3.00 bytes
Average Compression Size of a 12–Byte Key	5.75 bytes

Figure 2.11. Key compression example.

Based on the preceding information, the VSAM compression algorithm would have to reduce a 12–byte key to a size of 5.75 bytes on the average. VSAM uses the other 3 bytes to control the partial key in the index. This compression would occur at both ends of the key. What would happen if the algorithm did not compress to an average rate of 5.75 bytes but to a higher amount, say, 8.25 bytes? What actually occurs is that VSAM stops filling a CA the moment that it runs out of room in the index for another key. Thus all the CIs left in the CA are left empty from that point on. The next record is added into the first CI of the next CA and the process would start again. VSAM does not issue any warning message to alert the user of this condition. There are two ways in which the user can suspect that this is occurring. The first method is that the dataset uses secondary allocations when it is first loaded. Upon a review of the data, we find that the dataset is taking up much more space than it should. This is usually an indication of poor key compression. The second way that a user can suspect that there is a poor key compression is by using the output from a LISTCAT.

There is a field called "Freespc-Bytes" which can be used to help determine the possible key compression problem. "Freespc-Bytes" identifies the total space left over by all free control intervals in the dataset. Whenever poor key compression exists, an unusually high value in this field can be used as an indication of a potential problem. A simple method of determining this situation is to take the value at "Hi-Used-RBA" and subtract it from "Hi-Alloc-RBA." The result should be a figure close to the value found at "Freespc-Bytes." If this value is significantly higher than "Freespc-Bytes," a potential condition exists for poor key compression. A problem with this method occurs when the FSPC parameter at the CA level is used because entire free CIs reserved for FSPC are accounted in the total. However, the user can easily compute the requested CA FSPC amount and subtract it from the total.

As a starting point, anytime you are going to define a cluster that has a long key (e.g., more than 20 bytes), automatically be alert for the possibility of poor key compression. There are several alternative ways of getting VSAM to use all the CIs in the CA:

- Reduce the size of your CA, which directly reduces the number of CIs/CA. This is not a good solution.
- Increase the data CI size, which tends to reduce the number of CIs/CA and, thus reduce the number of keys required to fit in the index record. This solution depends on other considerations such as the availability of real/virtual storage and/or exclusive control contention.
- Increase the index CI size by specifying a larger value in the cluster definition at the index level. This is probably the best solution.

Poor key compression constitutes the first case where the specification of the index CI size at cluster definition is required to recover the space. The other cases are discussed in the next sections.

Controlling the Number of Index Levels

VSAM always has to have a single index record that is the high index record. We can almost think of this record as the commanding officer of the dataset. VSAM builds the index structure in the form of a pyramid, with the highest index at the top. A new index level is created whenever VSAM detects that there is more than one index record at what was the previous high level.

The lowest index level is called the sequence set. All other higher levels are collectively called the index set. Although VSAM looks at the indices as though they were in a hierarchical format, the indices are really written out as a flat file with the last index record being written at the end. The hierarchical logic is maintained by using the horizontal and vertical pointers located in the index records. The RBA location of the highest index record is kept in the catalog along with the cluster definition.

VSAM selects the index CI size depending on the number of CIs/CA. This means that VSAM expects to be able to compress a specified number of keys into a particular size CI. All index records are the same size regardless of whether they are sequence or index set records. One basic difference, however, between the index set record and sequence set record is the size of the control information required by index set to control the compressed keys. In some cases, this control information may be larger, and therefore fewer keys can potentially be stored in the data portion of the index set record. The actual number of compressed keys that will fit into the control interval depends on the effectiveness of the key compression at the time the index level records are created. For the purposes of this discussion, an equal number of estimated keys will be used as fitting into an index set and a sequence set record.

The sequence set record must be large enough to contain an entry per CI in each CA. As each new sequence set record is created, the high key from each sequence set record is saved in a second-level index. If the sequence set record has a capacity to store 55 keys (representing 55 CIs/CA), the second-level index should be large enough to store up to 55 compressed sequence set keys. This may be lower, as explained in the previous paragraph. Once the second-level index gets full, another second-level index record is created to accommodate the new sequence set keys. Since there are now two index records at the same level, VSAM now creates a third-level record to become the high-level index. This third-level index contains the high key of each second-level index set record. This process now continues as new records are added to the file. This third-level index could potentially accommodate up to 55 second-level key indices, depending on the effectiveness of the key compression.

Suppose we had an index CI size of 512 bytes. Figure 2.10 indicates that this size should accommodate 58 or fewer compressed keys. If the dataset is defined with each CA being the equivalent of one cylinder (or 744 FBA blocks), there would be a sequence set record for each cylinder of data. Logically, we can conclude that when the dataset reaches approximately 58 cylinders in size, the index set record will fill up, causing the creation of another second-level index set record and an additional index level and record. However, imagine that the dataset only occupied 60 cylinders. Then the file would have a three-level index structure because it exceeded 58 keys. In cases such as this, the user may opt to specify a larger index CI size than the VSAM default. Making the index CI size larger would probably not benefit the sequence set index, but it could benefit the index set because now more keys can be accommodated at this level, therefore, delaying the necessity to create the third-level index as in the example.

This technique is used quite often by people who continually review the VSAM datasets and determine that the file falls within the described circumstances. Note that the index record requires more storage than is needed to gain this benefit. This could be another reason why the user may decide to specify the index CI size for the dataset.

Forcing a Particular Index Size When Using an LSR Pool

Another reason for specifying the index CI size occurs when the dataset is used in a Local Shared Resource (LSR) pool. This normally occurs for online datasets. The user may want to force a particular CI size for the index to differentiate buffers reserved for the data and buffers reserved for the index. Chapter 9 contains an in-depth discussion of this point.

MVS Compatibility

One final reason for forcing a particular CI size is to maintain compatibility between DOS and MVS datasets. DOS index sizes can be significantly different for DOS from MVS (Pre-DFP 2.2). In particular, DOS indices can exceed the 4K–size limitation stipulated for MVS (Pre-DFP 2.2). If the dataset is to be accessible to MVS, the user must force an acceptable MVS index size. This is the final reason why a user could want to explicitly state the index CI size.

Recommendations for the Selection of the Index CI Size

In general terms, it is best to let VSAM select the CI size for the index. In those cases where the user notes either poor key compression and/or a specific dataset size characteristic where making the CI size larger would improve the performance of VSAM, the user should specify an index CI size in the cluster definition at the index level. A user should always review the index levels generated for a dataset. Too many index levels, especially for a small file, can indicate a poor definition, usually at either the data CI or CA size. Any changes made to the CI or CA size of a dataset involve the redefinition and reloading of the file.

PHYSICAL RECORD SIZE

One area that merits attention is the relationship between the selected CI size and the actual physical record size that VSAM selects. This discussion is valid for CKD units where the physical record size can vary the track utilization. FBA units are designed around a 512–byte sector and do not have the same type of considerations. There are some CI sizes for which VSAM creates a different physical record size. These CIs are read/written into/from storage with a single channel program, although it requires more chained CCWs. VSAM selects the physical block size based on the requested CI size. The chosen physical record size will be a multiple of the selected CI size.

Note that more resources are consumed in longer CCW programs. The objective, whenever selecting a CI size, is to ensure that the resulting CI size is equal to the physical record size. Even though the track utilization is improved, having to wait for additional gaps and control information to go by before reading the information makes the reading and/or writing of a CI slower than it would be for an equivalent size. Therefore, the user should ensure that the definition of the cluster uses a CI size that will generate a physical record of the same size as the CI being defined. Some suggested sizes can be found in Figures 2.2 and 2.3.

FBA Fragmentation

FBA devices are based on a sector size of 512 bytes. This size is ideally suited for VSAM CIs. Different from CKD units, which can lose space because of poor track utilization and incorrect CA size allocation, FBA losses due to poor CI sizes occur only at the end of CA. For example, suppose you define a CA size of 744 blocks. If a CI size of 4K bytes is requested, a total of 93 CIs is created. Each 4K CI requires 8 FBA blocks. Therefore, 744 blocks will accommodate 93 CIs completely (93 CIs/CA * 8 FBA Blocks/CI). However, if the requested CI size were 5K (10 FBA blocks), then you would obtain 74 CIs but would lose the last 4 FBA blocks or 2K.

CIs can span past "tracks" but not across CAs. As mentioned earlier, a 3370 disk unit is similar in characteristics to a 3375 disk unit. A 3375 has twelve tracks per cylinder. Note that a 3370 has 62 FBA blocks equivalent to one CKD track. If you multiply the 62 FBA blocks per "track" times the 12 "tracks per cylinder," you get the 744 FBA blocks representing the Max-CA size. This is the only type of loss created by the selection of CI size on an FBA device. A smaller CA size than the Max-CA size can have more dramatic losses, as can be seen in Figure 2.12.

	CASE 1		CASE 2	
Allocation Request	Blocks	(744 62)	Blocks	(744 744)
CA Size	62	Blocks	744	Blocks
CI Size	4	K	4	K
FBA Blocks/CI	8	Blocks	8	Blocks
# of CIs/CA	7	CIs/CA	93	CIs/CA
Lost Blocks/CA	6	Blocks/CI	0	Blocks/CA
Bytes Lost/CA	3	K Bytes	0K	Bytes/CA
Equivalent Byte Loss due to poor CA selection (744 Blocks) at Max-CA allocation	36	K Bytes	0K	Bytes
Max CIs/CA at 744 Blocks	84	CIs/CA	93	CIs/CA
Total Loss	9	CIs/CA	0	CIs/CA

Figure 2.12. FBA fragmentation loss.

MVS/XA Physical Record Size Selection

Newer releases of the DFP software have significantly changed the way VSAM selects the physical record size. VSAM can now select a physical record up to 32K bytes. In general, VSAM tries to make the physical record size equal to the CI size. In certain cases, VSAM recognizes that the physical record size will provide poor track utilization. In these cases, VSAM looks for a physical record size that will yield better track utilization. For example, on a 3380 disk unit a 12K CI will be converted into two 6K physical records. The reason is that a 12K physical record yields only a 36K byte track utilization (3 × 12K) with approximately 11K bytes lost. VSAM selects a physical record size of 6K, which yields a 42K byte track utilization, or a loss of approximately 5K bytes.

The importance of this change is that VSAM can now create a 22K physical record, which is good for sequential processing on a 3380. Also, two 22K records will fit on a track providing a 44K byte track utilization, or a loss of approximately 3K. This is the highest track utilization possible with VSAM. For direct processing, a 4–8K physical record is still valid.

Another advantage related to the change is that the index CI size can now be larger than 4K. This resolves the potential key compression problems whenever large keys are combined with a CA that contains a lot of CIs.

NEW DASD DEVICES

When computer manufacturers announce new DASD units the user must quickly establish what the minimum and maximum CA sizes are, regardless of whether the devise is a CKD or FBA unit. Also, the user should quickly determine what the best physical record and CI size combinations are so as to optimize the use of these new drives.

High Capacity DASD Units

Although the many new high-density DASD units announced are faster, the optimization process can be more complex. This results from having more data accessible by one access mechanism. Average seek is a term used to describe the amount of time it takes the access arm to transverse one-third of the cylinders on the drive. In the same length of time that it takes to transverse one-third of the cylinders on lower density drives, these new high-density DASD units will cover more cylinders. However, more datasets can be placed on these devices, therefore, increasing the amount of contention.

Part of the VSAM optimization deals with balancing the workload between these high-density drives. In some cases, this may require the underutilization of some DASD units. Since dataset distribution is a very important part of VSAM optimization, help from your systems programmer and/or DASD administrator is vital.

SUMMARY FOR CI SIZE SELECTION

When defining a cluster, always select the data CI size by specifying it at the data definition level in the AMS DEFINE command. Try to select a CI size that reflects your environment and the type of processing to be done. In general, a 4K CI size for data is good for most types of processing and disk devices. Larger CIs may be used for sequential processing. Under normal conditions let VSAM determine the size of the index CI. However, be alert for poor key compression or datasets with avoidable index levels when the index CI is larger. For those cases, specify the index CI size at the index level in the cluster definition. Also, be alert for datasets that have too many index levels, which can be an indication of either a poor data CI size or CA specification. Chapter 5 discusses how the CA size can be defined. Finally, try to select CI sizes that generate a same-size physical record to improve performance.

Chapter 3
FREE SPACE

The free space selection can have a positive or negative effect on VSAM performance. This chapter reviews the value of free space and under which circumstances free space should be allocated to the dataset. This is an important topic because indiscriminate use of free space can adversely affect total disk space utilization and total processing time.

THE CONCEPT OF FREE SPACE

When a dataset is created, the user should be aware of the dataset's characteristics. One of the important characteristics to consider is the dataset's volatility. This is the term that is used to describe whether or not records can be added or deleted in the processing cycle. As discussed in Chapter 1, the only VSAM organization where the RBA of the record could change was Key Sequence Dataset (KSDS). The term "Free Space" is used to refer to the area that is left inside the boundaries of the KSDS file to handle the addition of new records, or in the case of variable-length records, the expansion of the record. Free space is usually evenly distributed across the entire dataset even though there are techniques developed to load different parts of a dataset with different free space values. In those cases, the free space is evenly distributed across the dataset but at different specifications. This even distribution is an important fact to remember.

Free space can be reserved within a CI or by leaving a certain number of completely free CIs within a Control Area. The user specifies the amount of free space desired by using the FREE SPACE parameter in the AMS DEFINE command when creating the cluster or in the AMS ALTER command to change a prior specification for the cluster. The user explicitly requests this type of free space. Within a CI another type of available free space is created implicitly during the loading of the dataset. This type of free space is caused by not having a perfect record size that fits an even number of times into the CI after adjusting the space for the VSAM control information (RDF/CIDF). This type of free space can be called "dead weight" because it is normally not used unless variable-length records, which can be expanded in size, are being used. This type of free space can also be called CI fragmentation. Figure 3.1 is an example of this type of fragmentation.

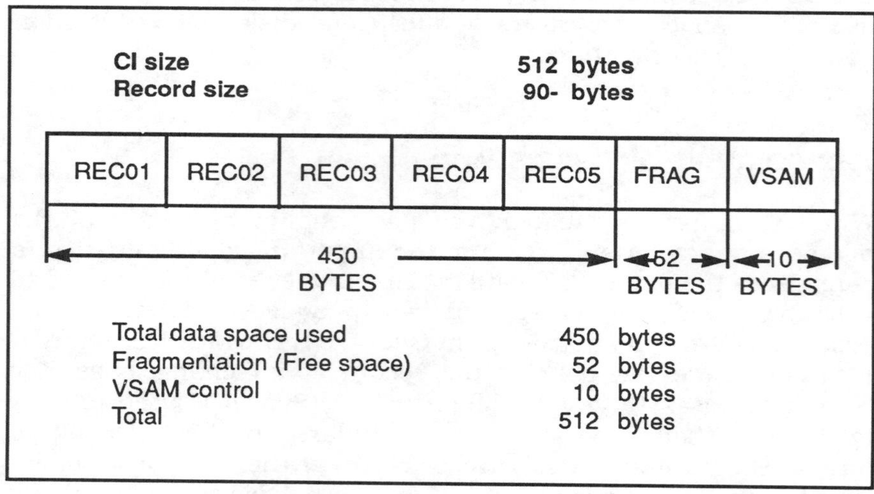

Figure 3.1. CI data fragmentation.

The user can explicitly request that free space be reserved by specifying a percentage figure to be used. There are two percentage values that the user could specify in the FSPC parameter of the IDCAMS DEFINE cluster. The first percentage indicates the amount of free space to be reserved within a CI. This value is multiplied by the CI size to determine the total number of bytes to be reserved. Note that even though the CI size is used, not all the bytes in the CI are available for data records. In order for the CI free space specification to be effective, enough room must be reserved in the CI to accept one data record.

VSAM always places at least one data record in each data CI regardless of the percentage specified for CI free space. In other words, you cannot use this percentage to create completely free CIs in a CA. If the user wants to be able to leave completely empty CIs within a CA for future expansion, the second percentage of the FSPC parameter should be used. This percentage is used to reserve a certain number of completely free or empty CIs within a CA. Note that the first free space parameter does not apply to the complete CIs reserved using the second free space parameter.

Free space is evenly distributed throughout the file. This important fact must be taken into consideration whenever deciding the value to be used. In order for a file to be able to fully utilize the free space that is evenly distributed, the additions or record expansions should also be evenly distributed throughout the file. This is not always the case in some files. For example, take a customer demand deposit account (checking account) in a bank. This file is usually kept in account number sequence. The first part of the account number usually identifies the branch. So, accounts are maintained in customer within branch sequence. New customers are added at the end of each branch. If the user specifies a free space value for this file, VSAM leaves that percentage across the entire file. Thus, a certain amount of free space is left that will never be used because records are never added in that section of the file.

There are some methods of loading a file with different free space specifications. One method is to use the option called KEYRANGES in the AMS cluster definition. In this manner a file can be broken down into smaller segments. Each segment can be loaded independently with a different free space value specified. This can be extremely cumbersome and slow if too many segments are involved. Most persons do not use this parameter for this purpose.

Another alternative is to load the file as compressed as possible by specifying zero free space. After the load is complete, the free space amount can be modified using the AMS ALTER command. Although this technique is mentioned in many VSAM manuals, its effectiveness in providing free space must be questioned. The moment that the first addition is made to the dataset, a CI/CA split is going to cause part of the records in the CI to be moved to a new CI. The number of records moved to the new CI depends on the type of processing being done to the file (e.g., sequential or direct) and where the new record was going to be inserted within the CI. The net effect is that a certain amount of free space is going to become available regardless of the free space percentage specified. The altering of the free space parameter may be useful when doing mass sequential insertions (MASSINSERT).

Positive Effects of Free Space

The main purpose of free space is to provide room for the addition of records and/or the expansion of variable-length records. By having sufficient free space available, the addition and/or expansion of records to the file will result in a faster operation. If insufficient space is not available, a CI and/or CA split can occur. This operation takes longer and the integrity of the dataset is exposed during this occurrence. The operation takes longer because additional I/O operations are required to write the new CIs and index records. The integrity is exposed because the index records have to be updated to adjust the horizontal and the vertical pointers within the index structure. Splits could occur in the index as a result of additions in the data that create additional keys to be held in the index record.

By having specified a certain amount of free space, the user can improve the overall performance of a dataset by reducing the exposure to splits. Splits are very time consuming and can affect online response when they occur. The dataset's integrity is also less exposed if there are no splits. The concept of CI and/or CA splits are discussed in Chapter 4.

Negative Affects of Free Space

Indiscriminate use of free space can have a negative effect on the performance of the VSAM dataset. The greater the amount of free space allocated, the greater the amount of DASD space the file will take up. This can also be translated into additional I/O operations, which increases the processing time for the dataset. These extra I/O operations involve additional supervisory, channel, and device times, which affect the overall performance of the system.

If a poor free space selection is combined with a poor CI size selection, the net result can have a direct negative effect on the performance of the dataset. The poor definition will affect the DASD space required, the number of I/Os required to process the file, and the number of index levels needed for the file.

FACTORS THAT CAN INFLUENCE THE FREE SPACE SPECIFICATION

The first determination to be made in the use of this parameter is whether or not it is needed. In other words, does this file receive any additions and/or record expansions? If the answer is no, do not specify any free space. If the answer is yes, the following questions must be answered:

- What is the growth of this dataset or how often is a record expanded?
- If the dataset is to receive additions, how are these additions distributed throughout the file? Are they evenly distributed? Are they inserted at the end of the dataset? Are they bunched in certain areas but not evenly distributed?
- How often do we plan to reorganize the dataset?
- Are there any deletions?

Many installations have a good handle on the volatility of a dataset. This should not be confused with the term"activity," which refers to how many records in a particular file must be accessed during the processing cycle. Most volatility statistics are carried on a yearly basis. That is, a dataset's growth rate is 10% per year. This is an important figure because it indicates how much free space must be provided for expansion on a yearly basis. Most growth rates for datasets are evenly distributed across a year, although there are peak type environments.

An important aspect is that this is a yearly figure and must be adjusted to reflect the frequency of dataset reorganizations. For example, if you have a dataset that has an annual growth of 12% and is reorganized every month, the actual total growth for the dataset is approximately 1% per month. Thus the computed free space must take this into consideration. Setting up a free space percentage of 12% for a dataset that is reorganized once a month may be too much for the return on investment. Therefore, you should set the free space percentage based on the dataset growth rate adjusted by the frequency of reorganizations.

One area that is usually not measured is the number of times that a record is expanded. These statistics are usually not available but form an important part in determining the free space percentage for a dataset, especially if there is a lot of activity in this area. Again, set the free space percentage adjusted to a reorganization cycle.

Another important consideration is to determine the distribution of these additions and/or expansions to the dataset. Where additions are evenly distributed, leaving both CI and CA free space will be useful. Where the additions may not be evenly distributed, leaving CA free space only may be the best solution. If you have a dataset that receives very little or no additions but does have record expansions, you should consider leaving CI free space only. If additions will occur only at the end of the file (EOF), leave no free space but allocate a larger primary space than required to handle these new records.

In summary, the use of free space depends on several factors. The use of free space at the CI level is best suited for additions that are evenly distributed throughout the dataset. For uneven distribution, the use of CA free space is best suited. A combination of both can provide the user with a certain degree of flexibility, which can cover both even and uneven record additions.

The Effect of Free Space Allocation

The FREESPACE (%CI %CA) parameter is used to instruct VSAM to leave a certain amount of free space available where the dataset is loaded or sequentially extended. FREESPACE can be specified as FSPC. The percentage specified is a whole number; that is, no fractions are permitted. When a CI percentage is specified, VSAM takes this percentage and multiplies it times the CI size to determine the amount of free space to be reserved. The product is truncated. The CA percentage is multiplied by the number of CIs in a CA to determine the number of completely free CIs that are going to be left empty in each CA. The product is truncated in MVS/XA. In DOS/VSE, the product is rounded up. In addition, in DOS/VSE, whenever the CA FSPC is specified (e.g., 1%), at least one CI is left free per CA. Figure 3.2 demonstrates these computations for a dataset on an IBM 3380 disk unit that has a CI size of 4096 bytes and a CA size of 1 cylinder.

CI Size	4096 Bytes
CI Free Space	10 Percent
Number of CI Free Space Bytes	409 Bytes
Number of CIs/CA	150 CIs/CA
CA Free Space	10 Percent
Number of Free CIs/CA	15 CIs/CA

Figure 3.2. CI/CA free space computation.

There is a certain amount of inconsistency in the free space percentages specified and the growth of the dataset. In the case of CI free space, the percentage specified should be large enough to cover the size of at least one logical record in the CI. Note that the growth of the dataset does not have any direct relationship to either the CI or record size. In fact, the user must be careful in selecting this free space percentage because the free space selected may not be large enough to accommodate one logical record. This is caused by the possible amount of fragmentation or "dead weight" in the CI. Figure 3.3 demonstrates a case where the free space percentage does not cover one logical record. No VSAM message is sent to alert the user to this fact.

The number of bytes left over as a result of fragmentation can affect the selection of the free space percentage. Whenever a free space amount is selected, VSAM places in the CI an imag-

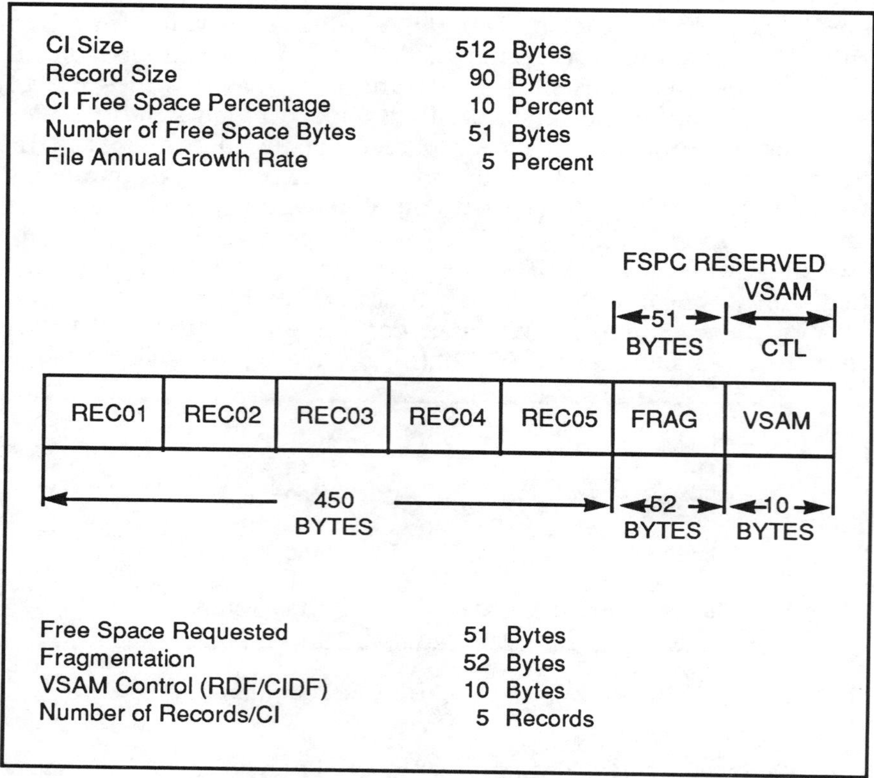

Figure 3.3. Effect of fragmentation on free space request.

nary line that is equal to the number of free space bytes displaced from the end of the VSAM control information. As the dataset is loaded, records are added to the CI until a record does not entirely fit without crossing the imaginary line. This record is placed into the next CI. If records are being inserted, a CI split would occur.

If the free space specification had been 11%, 56 bytes would have been requested. This would have exceeded the number of fragmented bytes. With this figure, the fifth logical record would not have fit into the CI without crossing the imaginary line. The net effect would have been to load four records into the CI leaving room for one addition. Note that this translates into a 20% free space allocation for a file that only has a 5% annual growth rate. This is the inconsistency in the free space allocation versus the actual growth rate.

The CA free space can also create an inconsistency when compared to an annual growth rate. The CA free space percentage is multiplied by the number of CIs/CA to determine the total number of completely empty CIs that are going to be left in each CA. Notice that this computation does not take into consideration the number of logical records actually reserved in the free CIs versus the real annual growth rate. Suppose you had a 10,000 record master file that was growing at a rate of 5% per year. This growth rate represents a growth of 500 new records during the first year. Figure 3.4 demonstrates the effect on an IBM 3380 Disk unit with a CI size of 512 bytes and a CA size of one cylinder.

Using the annual growth rate as a basis to establish the CA free space caused space for 680 records to be reserved. This represents an additional 180 records or an increase of approximately 36%. The actual percentage of growth reflected by 680 records is 6.8% per year. The actual amount of free space left is much larger because the dataset requires just a little over three CAs. In fact, if no free space had been specified, the dataset would have fit into three CAs. Thus the real effect of the 5% CA free space was to expand the dataset by 33%. Figure 3.5 reflects the combination of both CI and CA free space when applied to the dataset.

The net effect of requesting both CI and CA free space for the dataset is equivalent to reserving space for a 31.8% annual growth rate. Therefore, it is very important to compute the percentage required; otherwise, a very large amount of unused space can result. Also, note that this computation is based on an annual rate. If the file is reorganized on a weekly basis, the amount may be too high, which results in wasted DASD space and additional processing overhead. The CI sizes used in these examples were not typical but were used for the purpose of illustration. Larger CIs yield higher percentages because more logical records could fit into the free CIs.

The preceding figures also help to demonstrate the effect that free space has on DASD space and total I/O requirements for processing the file. Having to load an additional 500 CIs

CI Size	512	Bytes	
Record Size	90	Bytes	
File Annual Growth Rate	5	Percent	
CA Free Space Percentage	5	Percent	
Number of Records/CI Loaded	5	Records	
Number of CIs Required	2000	CIs	(10K recs/5 recs per CI)
Number of CIs/CA	690	CIs/CA	(46 CIs per trk * 15 trks)
Number of Free CIs/CA	34	CIs/CA	(690 CIs * .05 free space)
Number of Data CIs/CA	656	CIs/CA	(690 CIs – 34 CIs fspc)
Number of CAs Required for Load	4	CAs	(2000 CIs/656 CIs/CA) (rounded up)
Total Number of Free CIs	136	CIs	(34 CIs * 4 CAs)
Total Number of Free Records	680	Records	(136 CIs * 5 recs per CI)

Figure 3.4. Effect of free space reserved.

because of the free space requested plus leaving empty CIs within each CA had the effect of requiring more disk space and additional I/O operations to process the file. Note that no consideration was given to the dataset reorganization (load) process. If this dataset was reloaded weekly, the amount of space reserved was excessive.

Effect of Deletions on Free Space Selection

The number of deletions should be taken into consideration in adjusting the free space allocation under certain circumstances. VSAM recovers the deleted space in a CI immediately. However, the user must be aware if the deletion occurred in an area where additions can be made. If not, the number of deletions should not affect the amount of free space selected. If so, the user must factor this figure into the amount of free space requested. Note that a high number of deletions that result in unused space can be

CI Size	512	Bytes	
Record Size	90	Bytes	
Number of Free Space Bytes	102	Bytes	
File Annual Growth Rate	5	Percent	
CI Free Space Percentage	20	Percent	
CA Free Space Percentage	5	Percent	
Number of Records/CI (Max)	5	Records	
Number of Records/CI Loaded	4	Records	
Number of CIs Required	2500	CIs	(10K recs/4 recs per CI)
Number of CIs/CA	690	CIs/CA	(46 CIs per trk * 15 trks)
Number of Free CIs/CA	34	CIs/CA	(690 CIs * .05 free space)
Number of Data CIs/CA	656	CIs/CA	(690 CIs – 34 CIs fspc)
Number of CAs Required for Load	4	CAs	(2500 CIs/656 CIs/CA) (rounded up)
Total Number of Free CIs	136	CIs	(34 CIs * 4 CAs)
Number of Records in Free CIs	680	Records	(136 CIs * 5 recs per CI)
Number of Free Records per CI	2500	Records	(1 logical record per CI)
Total Number of Free Records	3180	Records	

Figure 3.5. Effect of CI/CA free space.

cause for reorganization of the dataset in order to recover the space. This is especially true if the dataset is receiving additions that are causing the file to expand.

POSSIBLE FREE SPACE SOLUTION TO UNEVEN DATASET INSERTIONS

It is unfortunate that the only direct way of specifying free space results in an even distribution of free space across a file. This has the negative effect of creating unusable space in the file. One technique that can be used is that of KEYRANGES, which is discussed in more detail in Chapter 7. In this manner, a dataset can be loaded in separate segments specifying different free space percentages. Although this may help somewhat, the process is manual and cumbersome. In addition, it does not lend itself to leaving free areas in between segments as would be required in a demand deposit accounting (checking) file.

An ideal parameter that would be extremely useful for VSAM datasets requiring uneven space distribution at specific locations would be something that would allow the insertion of "n" empty records at a user-specified control break. This control break would be similar to the control break structure (L1–L9, LR) available to RPG users. Since no such parameter is available in VSAM to simulate this RPG function, the user can create the situation by writing a simple load program that will determine control breaks and will insert dummy records (taking the last valid key and adding one) into the file for "n" number of records. Subsequently, the dummy records are deleted by the load program and the space made available for future insertions. This technique is very useful especially when the dummy keys are known ahead of time. The deleted space is automatically reclaimed by VSAM and available for immediate use. Depending on the operating system and VSAM version, completely empty CIs can be reclaimed as free CIs for future use. That is, the high key value can be reset and the free CI made available for any CI split.

RECOMMENDATIONS FOR FREE SPACE

When allocating a percentage for free space, the user should ensure that the free space requested is necessary. Allocating free space to a dataset that has no additions or record expansions is a waste of resources. The user is urged to review the growth rate for the dataset and adjust it to the number of records involved. At the CI level, the percentage should be high enough to ensure that at least one logical record fits into the CI. Beware of CI fragmentation and its effect on the free space reserved. Adjust the percentages used to reflect the frequency of dataset reorganization and any applicable record deletions.

As a general rule, CI free space is best suited for evenly distributed additions or record extensions, whereas CA free space is best suited for uneven distribution. If record expansions are a possibility, consider using CI free space. If a dataset is to receive many additions, allocate both CI and CA free space. This is true for a dataset that is updated online. CA splits can result in variances of response times of several seconds depending on the workload. Online datasets should avoid CA splits.

As a final review, the user should analyze whether or not a specification of a lower free space can be offset by more frequent reorganizations of the dataset. The loading of the dataset is sequential, and good buffering techniques can make the load times faster. The net effect may be better space utilization with a lower overhead. Buffering is discussed in Chapter 6.

In summary, be very judicious in the use of the free space parameter when allocating a dataset. Set the free space percentage realistically to the growth expected. Overallocation can have a negative effect on performance by requiring too many resources for the entire dataset. Underallocation can have a negative effect if splits occur in the processing of the dataset, especially if it is an online dataset. A proper balance is required between the two.

Chapter 4
CI/CA SPLITS

CI and CA splits are usually a result of not having sufficient space to insert a record at a particular point in a dataset. The resulting performance issues caused by splits are the main topic of this chapter.

CI/CA SPLITS

CI and CA splits occur only in KSDS files where the RBA of the record can be changed. A CI split occurs when the data that is to be written does not fit into the CI. This frequently occurs to datasets that have insertions or additions made. The split can also occur when a variable-length record is expanded and there isn't sufficient room in the CI to accommodate the extension. Theoretically you can produce a CI split by decreasing the size of a record. This can happen if the data in the CI is compactly packaged into the CI with records so that no free space is available. One of the records in the CI is shortened by a small amount, and this breaks the length sequence in the RDF structure. This creates additional RDFs. Since no more free space is available, a CI split would have to occur to accommodate new RDFs. There is a possibility that this can occur, but it is very remote.

When a CI split occurs, VSAM searches within the current CA to find a completely empty CI to accommodate part of the records. If one is found, the contents of the original CI are split with the new CI. Both CIs are written into the CA. This requires updating the index CI to reflect this split. The IMBED and/or REPLICATE specification can also cause additional overhead because a full track or 62 FBA blocks containing the index record must be updated. This also elongates channel and device busy times. Splits take extra I/O operations and during a certain period, the integrity of the file is exposed to an external outage. As a final note on CI splits, a record addition into a CI could result in multiple CI splits in one operation. This can occur in datasets that have a wide variance in record lengths. Suppose that a densely packed CI receives an insertion of a very large record, which is almost as large as the CI. Even after the initial split, there still may not be enough space for the insertion of the large record. VSAM will continue to do splits until the record can be accommodated. This may also result in CA split.

If no free CI is found within the CA, a CA split occurs. VSAM will now try to locate a completely free CA at the end of the dataset in order to split the records between the CAs. If an available CA is found, part of the records in the original CA are written to the new CA, leaving space in both CAs for future additions. VSAM then proceeds to do the CI split that caused the CA split to occur. The CA split requires rewriting the original index record, reflecting the split, and adding a new index record at the end of the index extent. In addition, the catalog must also be updated to reflect the effect of the new CA. There is also a possibility that the index area may require an additional extent if the new index record does not fit into the current index space. This also requires catalog access and update. The REPLICATE and/or IMBED specification can also cause additional overhead for processing the index area since each index record is allocated a track, or 62 FBA blocks. This can cause additional overhead because a full track, or 62 FBA blocks, must be rewritten, creating a very long update. This elongates channel and device busy times. At certain points during this process, the dataset integrity is exposed.

One additional performance issue associated with CI/CA splits is that while a split is occurring, no other activity can occur against the dataset until the split has completed. That means that all activity is "single threaded" until the split completes. This affects use in an online environment. The reason that the requests must be single threaded is that while the indices are being updated as a result of split, VSAM must protect them against another update of the indices.

If there is no free CA at the end of the file, a new extent must be acquired if the file extent limits have not been exceeded. This requires going into the catalog and/or VTOC (ICF catalogs or unique datasets) to find additional space as well as updating the catalog and/or VTOC (ICF catalogs or unique datasets) with the new information. The locating of an additional extent may also occur if the current index extent is full and an additional index record is to be written. If additional space is not available, the addition is not done and a return code is returned to the user. Space may not be available because:

- No secondary allocation was specified.
- The dataset's extent limit was reached.
- There is no more physical space left on the volume or VSAM space and no other candidate volumes were specified.

The number of extents available to a dataset varies by the specifications defined for the dataset. Normally a VSAM dataset has a total capacity of 123 extents. The REUSE and/or UNIQUE specification causes the total number of extents to be reduced to 16 per volume. Datasets defined under an ICF catalog environment appear as unique in the LISTCAT although the user did not request the unique attribute. However, in these cases, the dataset is still allowed 123 extents.

Remember that VSAM can use up to five extents to satisfy a primary or secondary request. The number used to satisfy a primary or secondary allocation will reduce the total number of available extents by the number of extents used to satisfy the allocation request.

As can be seen from the preceding discussion, the occurrence of CI and/or CA splits can negatively affect performance, exposing the dataset's integrity while the split occurs. Datasets that contain a high number of CI and/or CA splits are candidates for reorganization. The free space allocation and reorganization frequency should also be analyzed.

Additional Negative Effects of CI/CA Split

In addition to taking up more processing time when the split occurs, the occurrence of splits in a dataset can also affect its processing in the future. If the file is processed sequentially, the presence of splits in the file will elongate the processing time because additional CIs must be read. Split CAs are located at the end of the dataset, forcing an arm movement. If the dataset is processed directly, no significant overhead should result from having to locate the record unless the index record is located in a different extent. Additional extents caused by CA splits could result in additional virtual storage usage in the processor storage for the control blocks that carry this information.

Another negative effect of CI/CA splits is that the resulting free space inside the CI or the CA is not used because the key numbers within the range are already used up. This space can only be recovered by a reorganization where the space is recompacted. An example of this is given in Figure 4.1.

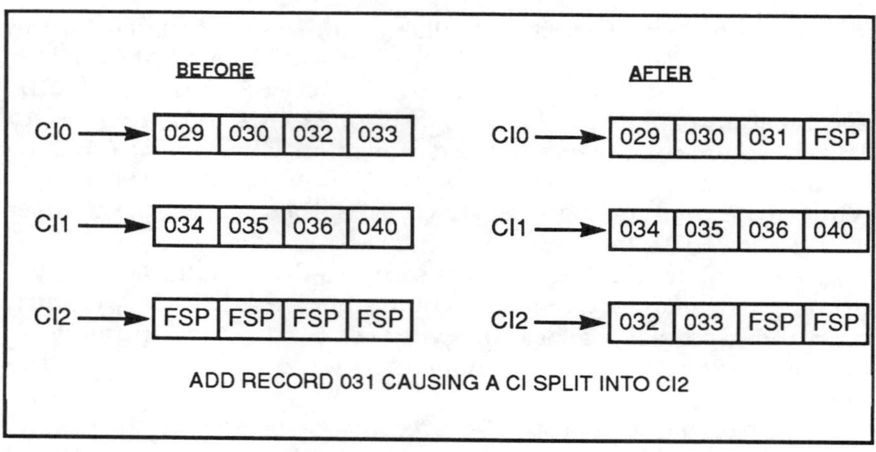

Figure 4.1. The effect of splits on available free space.

Figure 4.1 depicts the negative effect created by a CI split with regards to the unused free space created. The free space created in CI0 and CI2 cannot be used because no valid key could be inserted into either CI. This extra space now creates an overhead in processing that will only be relieved by a reorganization of the file. The CI may be able to accommodate lower key values, depending on the high key of the previous CI.

Users of the IMBED and/or REPLICATE options may experience longer delays whenever a CI or a CA split occurs. This is so because, in both of these options, each index record is repeated the number of times that it will fit into a track, or 62 FBA blocks. In the case of IMBED, the sequence set record occupies the first track of the data CA. In the case of REPLICATE, each index set record and sequence set record (if IMBED is not specified) occupies its own track in the index area. Therefore, any changes to the index record result in having to update a full track of indices instead of one record. This takes at least one revolution of the disk unit. These two index options are discussed in Chapter 8.

CI/CA Split Strategy

Up to now we have more or less assumed that each time a split occurs, one-half of the records are moved to the new area. VSAM has two strategies for performing splits:

1. Normal Insert Strategy (NIS) — This procedure is used when the dataset is being processed in direct mode.
2. Sequential Insert Strategy (SIS) — This procedure is used when the dataset is being processed in sequential mode.

In NIS mode, the split occurs at the half way point of either the CI or CA to be split. In this mode, half of the records are moved to the new CI or CA, regardless of where the insertion was to take place. In SIS mode, the split occurs at the logical insertion point of the new data. This means that if the key to be inserted is higher than any other key, the key becomes the first record of the new CI or CA. If it is not the highest key, the new record is placed in the old CI/CA with all records containing a higher key going into the new CI/CA.

The actual number of records moved depends on which strategy is being used at the time that the addition or expansion is made. The movement of data from one CA to the next is accomplished through chained I/O operations to improve the performance and time required. The use of chained I/O operations depends on the type of buffer resources being used. Non-Shared Resources (NSR) use chained I/O operations while performing the CA split. Local Shared Resources (LSR) do not perform chained I/O operations. If a dataset has heavy CA split activity, the use of NSR could be more efficient. CA splits are single threaded.

REORGANIZATION VERSUS SPLITS

Splits can be used as a sign that a file needs to be reorganized. In general terms, CI splits with no CA splits are no great cause for alarm or an indication that the file must be reorganized. Since CI splits remain within the same CA, access to these "out of physical sequence" CIs usually involves electronic head switching. CI splits with no CA splits should only be taken as an indication that a CA split may be a near possibility. Therefore a closer observation should be maintained of this file until it is reorganized.

There are times when a CI split can be more costly than just electronic head switching. This occurs when the user defines a CA size that is less than a cylinder, but the number of tracks selected is not a multiple of the number of tracks in a cylinder or the space allocated is not on a cylinder boundary. If this occurs, some additional arm movement is possible because a CA is split across two separate cylinders. For example, an IBM 3380 DASD unit has 15 tracks to a cylinder. If for some reason the selected CA size happens to be 10 tracks, the first cylinder of the 3380 will contain one whole CA and one-half of the next CA. The other half will be located at the beginning of the next cylinder.

Note that noncylinder space allocations are not necessarily cylinder aligned. VSAM space algorithms use a "best fit" method for DOS/VSE, VSE/SP, OS/VS1 and MVS non ICF catalogs. For MVS ICF catalogs, the space allocation is performed by DADSM, which uses a "first fit" algorithm. Since VSAM reserves CA free space at the end of a CA, there is a high probability of having to move the arm, especially if the IMBED option is used. Another major concern of CI splits should be the amount of unusable free space that may result from these splits. A possible guideline to use is: when the number of CI splits exceeds 20% of the CAs in the dataset, the dataset should be reorganized.

CA splits, on the other hand, are more serious than CI splits because larger amounts of data have been moved and there is the potential effect on performance as described earlier. The user should watch for CA splits that cause secondary allocations. Secondary allocations require more time and virtual storage to process. Datasets with this type of CA split should be reorganized soon. A common guideline is: when the number of CA splits exceeds 5% of the total CAs or when the dataset spans more than ten extents, the dataset should be reorganized.

A reorganization at this point is recommended because of the possible volume fragmentation caused by these extra extents and the possible extra arm movement when processing the dataset sequentially. Also, datasets that have been specified with the UNIQUE and/or REUSE options can only have 16 extents per volume. As in the case of CI splits, there is a possibility that additional unusable free space is created with these splits.

Recommendations for CI/CA Splits

The best alternative to reduce CI and CA splits is to allocate a certain amount of free space to the file. This was discussed in Chapter 3. The information regarding the number of CI and/or CA splits is maintained in the catalog where the dataset is defined. It should be periodically reviewed by using the AMS LISTCAT command. There are times when a few splits are going to occur. These should be planned. When the number of CI/CA splits exceeds a certain established installation threshold, the dataset should be reorganized. Too many splits increase the processing overhead and disk space requirements.

When a split occurs, the integrity of the dataset is in danger during certain parts of the split process. Therefore, reducing this exposure will indirectly help improve the dataset's integrity and availability. All datasets should be reviewed at least once a month. New datasets or volatile datasets should be reviewed initially on a weekly or biweekly basis. Areas to be reviewed include the initial primary allocation, CI/CA splits, and free space allocation.

Chapter 5
CONTROL AREA (CA) SIZE

This chapter focuses on the importance that the Control Area size has on performance in a KSDS file. Since the CA size is selected indirectly, there is a tendency to define its size incorrectly. The reasons and means of defining the largest CA size possible is the thrust of this chapter.

HOW IS THE CONTROL AREA SIZE DEFINED?

The Control Area is one of the building blocks of a VSAM dataset. It is used to define a collection of CIs in the dataset. The size of a CA is most important when discussing KSDS files. A CA can be as small as one track on a CKD disk unit or 62 blocks in an FBA disk unit. A CA can be as large as one cylinder in a CKD disk unit or 744 blocks in an FBA disk unit. The size of the CA is indirectly selected by the user when a cluster is defined. There is no parameter at the cluster definition that defines the CA size, as one would expect. VSAM determines the CA size using the primary and secondary space request. Some special VSAM parameters or requests can affect the CA size, and, in some cases, the hardware characteristics of the device being used for the definition can also affect the CA size selected. When changing DASD devices, the CA size is one area in which the performance may be adversely affected. This makes hardware changes less transparent than the user is led to believe.

Several methods are available for users to select the space allocation for a dataset. For CKD devices, the user can specify that the allocation be made in TRACKS, CYLINDERS, or RECORDS. For FBA devices, the user can specify that the allocation be made in BLOCKS or RECORDS. By far the most problematic in determining the CA size is the selection of space by means of the RECORD Specification. Unfortunately, this is the common method because most users know how many records are in the file but do not know how to translate this into tracks, cylinders, or blocks. To fine tune VSAM, the user must know how to do these conversions. Appendix B demonstrates several examples that can be used to determine the dataset size.

Chapter 1 describes the method that VSAM uses to allocate a dataset's CA size. A review of this figure may be helpful for the following discussion. Figure 1.9 has been repeated as Figure 5.1 for your review.

In some cases, VSAM overrides the user's specification due to some type of inconsistency in the user definition. For example, suppose that the user requests a primary allocation of one track and in the same definition requests that the dataset have IMBED specified. Since the first track will hold the dataset's sequence set, VSAM automatically adds one track to ensure that there will be at least one data track besides the sequence set. Another example is when the user requests a very large CI size and then proceeds to allocate a small primary quantity that will not hold the requested CI size. VSAM again increases the size to accommodate the CI size. In both of the cases mentioned, VSAM does not issue a warning message to alert the user. The only way of noticing this change in the allocation is by analyzing a LISTCAT printed output.

In the definition of a KSDS file, the size of the Control Area is very important. There is one index record per CA called a sequence set record. It is imperative for most KSDS files to have the CA size set to the largest value possible. This is one of the main tuning concerns for a KSDS file. The examples of CA size selections in Figure 5.1 should be reviewed to illustrate the relationship between the primary and secondary allocations.

	REQUESTED CLUSTER ALLOCATION	WHERE WAS THE REQUEST MADE?	WAS EMBED SPECIFIED?	OPERATING SYSTEM	ACTUAL CLUSTER ALLOCATION	CONTROL AREA SIZE (TRACKS)	COMMENTS
1.	TRACKS (100 3)	DATA	NO	MVS/XA ICF	TRACKS (102 3)	3	PRIMARY ADJUSTED (UP)
	TRACKS (100 3)	DATA	NO	DOS/VSE	TRACKS (103 3)	3	PRIMARY ADJUSTED (UP)
2.	TRACKS (100 3)	CLUSTER	YES	MVS/XA ICF	TRACKS (100 4)	4	SECONDARY ADJUSTED (UP)
	TRACKS (100 3)	CLUSTER	YES	DOS/VSE	TRACKS (99 3)	3	PRIMARY ADJUSTED (DOWN)
3.	TRACKS (100 3)	CLUSTER	NO	MVS/XA ICF	TRACKS (99 3)	3	PRIMARY ADJUSTED (DOWN)
	TRACKS (100 3)	CLUSTER	NO	DOS/VSE	TRACKS (99 3)	3	PRIMARY ADJUSTED (DOWN)
4.	TRACKS (1 1)	CLUSTER	YES	MVS/XA ICF	TRACKS (2 2)	2	PRIMARY/SECONDARY ADJUSTED (UP)
	TRACKS (1 1)	CLUSTER	YES	DOS/VSE	TRACKS (2 2)	2	PRIMARY/SECONDARY ADJUSTED (UP)
5.	TRACKS (2 2)	CLUSTER	YES	MVS/XA ICF	TRACKS (3 3)	3	PRIMARY/SECONDARY ADJUSTED (UP)
	TRACKS (2 2)	CLUSTER	YES	DOS/VSE	TRACKS (2 2)	2	NO CHANGE
6.	TRACKS (3)	CLUSTER	NO	MVS/XA ICF	TRACKS (6 3)	3	PRIMARY ADJUSTED (UP)
	TRACKS (5 3)	CLUSTER	NO	DOS/VSE	TRACKS (6 3)	3	PRIMARY ADJUSTED (UP)
7.	TRACKS (5 3)	CLUSTER	YES	MVS/XA ICF	TRACKS (4 4)	4	PRIMARY/SECONDARY ADJUSTED (DOWN/UP)
	TRACKS (5 3)	CLUSTER	YES	DOS/VSE	TRACKS (6 3)	3	PRIMARY ADJUSTED (UP)
8.	TRACKS (100 3)	DATA	YES	MVS/XA ICF	TRACKS (100 4)	4	SECONDARY ADJUSTED (UP)
	TRACKS (100 3)	DATA	YES	DOS/VSE	TRACKS (102 3)	3	PRIMARY ADJUSTED (UP)
9.	TRACKS (97 3)	DATA	NO	MVS/XA ICF	TRACKS (98 7)	7	PRIMARY ADJUSTED (UP)
	TRACKS (97 7)	DATA	NO	DOS/VSE	TRACKS (88 7)	7	PRIMARY ADJUSTED (UP)
10.	TRACKS (97 7)	DATA	YES	MVS/XA ICF	TRACKS (104 8)	8	PRIMARY (SECONDARY ADJUSTED (UP/UP)
	TRACKS (97 7)	DATA	YES	DOS/VSE	TRACKS (98 7)	7	PRIMARY ADJUSTED (UP)

Figure 5.1. Sample CA size calculations.

Using the RECORDS Parameter to Reserve VSAM Space

One of the most difficult ways to control the CA size allocation is to use the RECORDS parameter in the cluster definition. The reason for this is that VSAM does not account for the free space requested nor the effect of the IMBED option, where you lose the first track, or 62 blocks, of every CA in the file. If the file contains variable-length records, VSAM uses the average record length specification to compute the requested amount. In too many instances, users interpret this figure to mean the smallest record and not the most common, or "mode" in statistical terms. The average is the requested amount, but the average can be misleading. A true average can only be found by multiplying the varying lengths by the number of occurrences. Therefore, we recommend using the mode. In many cases where this value is set incorrectly, the file takes up additional secondary extents when loaded. To compensate for this shortcoming, many users increase the number of records in the file to fool VSAM into giving the dataset more space.

The use of the RECORDS parameter to allocate space also has a negative effect when specifying the secondary allocation. Many users use a "golden rule" of 10% of the primary records or, in some cases, the file growth rate in order to select the secondary quantity. Using this "golden rule"' on small- to medium-sized datasets can adversely affect the CA size selected by VSAM. It is highly recommended that datasets that use this method of requesting space be closely monitored until the CA size is adjusted to the highest value possible.

PRIMARY AND SECONDARY ALLOCATION

Whenever possible, specify the primary and secondary allocation requests in cylinders for CKD devices and multiples of 744 blocks for FBA devices. This forces the allocation of the dataset on a cylinder boundary and forces the CA size to one cylinder. Unless specifically told not to do so, all dataset allocations should include a primary and a secondary value. This ensures that any error in the primary allocation will be covered by a secondary request.

If the requested amount is less than one cylinder, or 744 FBA blocks, make the primary and secondary request of the same size. This ensures the largest CA size possible for the data. It is imperative to remember that the secondary request does not have any effect on space reservation until it is needed. However, the secondary request may be influential in determining the CA size, for example, a dataset of less than one cylinder in size.

For a KSDS file, it is very important to set the CA size to the highest value possible. The guide should be to have the CA size equal to a max-CA. In the cases where the file is smaller than the max-CA value, it is imperative to set the CA size to the maximum possible size for the file. The reason is very simple. There is one sequence set record for every CA in the file. If the CA size is set too small, the number of sequence set records increases over the required number. As an example, let us review Figure 5.2.

DESCRIPTION	FILE A	FILE B
Allocation	Tracks (7 1)	Tracks (7 7)
CA Size	1 Track	7 Tracks
Number of Sequence Set Records	7 Records	1 Record
Number of Index Set Records	1 Record	0 Records
Total Number of Index Records	8 Records	1 Record
Total Number of Index Levels	2 Levels	1 Level

Figure 5.2. Effect of CA size on indices.

Several interesting facts can be seen in the preceding definition. The most glaring item is the effect that a poor CA size has on a KSDS file. By making the CA size very small, the file required two levels of indices and a total of eight records. This is computed by having one sequence set record per CA, and since there is more than one index record at the same level, a higher level was required to control the lower level. This results in seven sequence set records plus one index set record. To process this file in a direct method, assuming no additional index buffers, a total of two index reads plus one data read would be required. Each subsequent read would require the index set record to be reread followed by a read to the sequence set record. This item could be reduced by increasing the number of index buffers in storage at a cost of virtual and real storage. File B requires that the index be read only on the first read followed by the read for the data. Subsequent reads do not require the reading of the index since it is still in storage at no additional cost than the minimum for reading the file.

For sequential processing, File A would require the reading of the index set record followed by the reading of each sequence set record to locate the data. When processing sequentially, the sequence set records are not read ahead, which forces a wait after each CA is processed in order to retrieve the next sequence set record. File B, on the other hand, only requires that the first and only index record be read into storage. From there all the tracks in the CA are accessible at no additional cost.

As can be seen from the preceding example, any KSDS file that is less than the max-CA size should be forced to have the primary and secondary allocation requests be the same. This forces a CA size equivalent to the maximum that can be allocated for a small file. The main concern would be if there is enough space to allocate the secondary amount. With quantities this small, there should be no problem. The secondary amount plays no part in the initial allocation of the primary amount. Therefore, making the primary and the secondary quantities the same should not have any effect on the allocation but will greatly enhance the performance of the dataset.

If your installation uses the RECORDS parameter to reserve space for the files, ensure that the specification for the secondary amount is equal to the primary amount in those cases where the primary request is less than one cylinder. In those cases where your request is close to a cylinder boundary, it is best to round off to a cylinder so that VSAM can use multitrack operations without having to test for the end of the file (EOF) after every track. The use of the CYL parameter reduces the fragmentation experienced on a disk that has many TRACKS type specifications. The use of the TRACKS parameter does not guarantee that the dataset will be cylinder-aligned even if the total tracks requested exceed one cylinder.

The CA Size and Its Effect on CA Free Space Percentage (DOS/VSE)

As discussed in Chapter 3, the CA free space percentage is multiplied by the number of CIs in a CA to determine how many free CIs are going to be left for future use. The product of this multiplication is truncated in MVS/XA but rounded up in DOS/VSE. However, whenever a CA FSPC percentage is requested (e.g., 1%) in DOS/VSE, at least one free CI/CA is reserved, regardless of the product. Making the CA size small can have a negative effect in this area by leaving a larger number of free CIs than was expected due to this process. This means that, given an equivalent space where CA free space has been specified, the file with the smaller CA can result in having more free space reserved. Figure 5.3 demonstrates this effect for an IBM 3350 disk unit.

SPECIFICATION	FILE A	FILE B
CA Size	1 Track	1 Cylinder
CI Size	1024 Bytes	1024 Bytes
CA Free Space	1%	1%
Number of CIs/CA	15 CIs/CA	450 CIs/CA
Number of Free CIs/CA	1 CI/CA	5 CIs/CA
For 30 Tracks (Equivalent)	30 CIs/CA	5 CIs/CA

Note
For an equivalent amount of tracks, there is an increase of 26% CIs/CA of FSPC.

Figure 5.3. Effect of the CA size on the CA free space request.

As can be seen from the preceding example, the setting of the CA size to an incorrect value coupled with a request for CA free space can result in leaving a much larger free space than anticipated. This excess space affects performance, as discussed in Chapter 3. This is another reason why care must be taken when determining the CA size of the file.

Imbed and the CA Size

Another consideration is the use of IMBED in the cluster definition. The effect of IMBED on a small CA size can also be negative on performance. IMBED is a means by which the sequence set record is placed on the first track of the data CA, or the first 62 FBA blocks. The track is completely used because the sequence set record is repeated whatever number of times it will fit on the track. This is called replication. On devices that had a great number of tracks per cylinder, IMBED had a minimal effect on the total capacity of the CA.

For example, an IBM 3350 has 30 tracks per cylinder. If IMBED is specified, the user would lose only 1/30 of a cylinder to the index portion. This comes out to approximately 3.33% of the total CA capacity. The remainder would be dedicated to data. In the case of an IBM 3375, which has only 12 tracks per cylinder, the use of IMBED results in the loss of 1/12 of the CA, or 8.25%. The total effect in total bytes can also be much higher in the newer high-capacity drives.

Imagine the effect of specifying a CA size equivalent to two tracks for a 3375. This would mean that 50% of the CA capacity would go to handle the sequence set record. This not only would result in poor space utilization but would negate any performance improvement that could have been gained by specifying IMBED.

Therefore, if the use of IMBED is necessary, the size of the CA should be set to the max-CA specification order to minimize the effect that IMBED has on the CA data capacity. If the CA size is set too small, the overall effects to the space required and time to process the file could be so negative they would negate the use of IMBED. Note that IMBED is unnecessary for datasets that occupy less than one cylinder as seen in Figure 5.2. In these cases there is nothing to be gained by the use of IMBED when the CA size is set to the maximum CA size possible. This will ensure one index record for the dataset. If we set the value of the CA size for a small dataset (one that is less than one cylinder, or 744 blocks) to the maximum size, there will be only one index record. Since one index buffer is reserved, this record would always be in storage, negating any access improvements that IMBED would provide.

Secondary Allocations

One area that should be addressed is how large the secondary allocation should be made. In the case of files that are less than one cylinder, or 744 blocks, the secondary quantity should equal the primary amount. In those other cases where the primary amount is going to result in a max-CA allocation, the secondary quantity should not be set to a small amount; nor should it be set to a large amount, which may cause cancellations due to lack of disk space.

The idea behind the secondary allocation requires some explanation. As mentioned earlier, the secondary allocation is not reserved until all of the primary space is exhausted. The secondary allocation is requested when the primary allocation is underestimated or when the file has received so many additions that there have been many CA splits or dataset extensions. To obtain a secondary space, VSAM has to almost effectively go through a similar process of an "open" routine. This takes a lot of time in the system and the disk units involved. If you set the secondary allocation too small and the file requires more space than requested, VSAM has to go through the overhead of "opening" the file repeatedly. This creates an overhead that affects system throughput. If, instead, the secondary allocation is set at a higher value, the price for negotiating another CA would be spread out across more space.

As an example, let us use a file where we have specified a secondary allocation of one cylinder. If the file requires 10 secondary cylinders, VSAM would have to go through the secondary allocation routine ten times. Each of these allocations would also involve access to the catalog and/or VTOC (Volume Table of Contents). If, instead, the secondary allocation is set at ten cylinders, VSAM would go through the secondary allocation routine once. The first example would have resulted in ten additional extents, which could have been critical if the file was approaching the extent maximum. The second example could have resulted in only one extent if ten contiguous cylinders were available.

The major concern for having a large secondary request is the possible lack of space on the volume to satisfy the request. VSAM is designed to try to obtain the requested amount in up to five extents, just as the primary. The idea is to request an amount that, if required, will not expose the user to lack of space while at the same time reducing the amount of secondary allocations required for the file. Figure 5.4 provides some guidelines that can be used in setting up the secondary allocations of larger files. For FBA devices, multiply the amount in cylinders by 744 blocks.

FILE SIZE	SUGGESTED SECONDARY
001–005 Cylinders	1 Cylinder
006–020 Cylinders	2 Cylinders
021–050 Cylinders	5 Cylinders
051–100 Cylinders	10 Cylinders
101–200 Cylinders	15 Cylinders
201–300 Cylinders	20 Cylinders
301+ Cylinders	25 Cylinders

Figure 5.4. Suggested secondary allocations.

RECOMMENDATIONS FOR THE CA SIZE SELECTION

It is the primary objective of all KSDS users to make the CA size of a file equal to the max-CA size of the disk unit being used. This will reduce the number of index records and, in some cases, index levels associated with this file. If the file occupies less than the max-CA, it is best to set the CA size equal to the highest allocation requested. This is done by requesting the same quantity for both the primary and secondary allocations. For this type of dataset, do not specify IMBED since the CA size can be made to have one index record to control the entire CA. Also, be sure that the CA size requested is a multiple of the number of tracks available on the device. This ensures that the CA is self-contained in one cylinder and does not overflow into another cylinder, causing additional arm movement. If the requested amount is close to one cylinder, round it off to a cylinder boundary to enhance I/O operations through the use of multitrack operations.

Finally, when requesting secondary space, do not be meek. Request an amount that will reduce the cost of having to process future secondary allocations.

Chapter 6
I/O BUFFER ALLOCATION

An important performance option is buffer space allocation. The VSAM default buffer allocation is inadequate for the majority of datasets. This chapter focuses on I/O buffer space selection based on the processing mode of the dataset.

GENERAL I/O ALLOCATION CONCEPTS

A VSAM cluster requires allocating main storage space to process the dataset, which is called an Input/Output Area, or I/O area for short. The amount of storage to be allocated can be explicitly defined by the user, left to default, or selected by VSAM. The actual amount of storage defaulted depends on whether the cluster is a KSDS or an ESDS/RRDS file. In all cases, VSAM defaults to two I/O areas for the data portion of the cluster. In the case of a KSDS, VSAM defaults to one I/O area for the index portion of the cluster. The amount of storage required to process the dataset can be found in a LISTCAT of the cluster under the title BUFSPACE.

The user may override the VSAM default in several places. The first place where the user could allocate more space than the VSAM default is at cluster definition time. During the definition, the user could specify a greater amount than the default value. A second area where the user could override the I/O area requirements is in the definition of the ACB (Access Control Block) at open time. Another area where the user could specify the amount of storage required for the I/O areas is in the JCL using the AMP parameter of the // DD card (OS) or in the // DLBL card (DOS). The most common method is to specify the required amount through the JCL. One final method is to run an AMS ALTER command and change the assigned BUFSPACE.

I/O Area Assignment

The storage areas required to process the file are allocated when the file is opened for processing. These areas are released when the file is closed. Buffer areas are aligned on page boundaries for the data portion and for the index portion, if present. VSAM uses the buffers employing the Least Recently Used (LRU) algorithm. The buffer usage varies, depending on the type of processing to be performed. When processing the file sequentially, SHAREOPTIONS 1–3 allows VSAM to read ahead if sufficient buffers are allocated. SHAREOPTIONS 4 does not permit VSAM to read ahead no matter how many buffers are allocated.

Index buffers are loaded or read only when they are used. Therefore, no read-ahead capability is allowed in the index area. As mentioned earlier, VSAM takes the allocated buffer space and divides it among the necessary buffer types, depending on the processing options specified. For example, if the dataset is to be processed sequentially, the user would want to have more data buffers allocated so that VSAM could use the read-ahead features to overlap processing with I/O operations. If the dataset is to be processed directly, the user would want to have fewer data buffers and more index buffers to maintain the greatest number of index records in storage to accelerate the access to the requested record.

The number and type of buffers required is the determination that the user would have to make. Since a dataset's processing requirements vary, it is better to specify the required buffer space through the JCL. This provides maximum flexibility because the buffer space can be temporarily altered for the duration of the program.

JCL SPECIFICATION FOR BUFFER SPACE IN MVS

In MVS the Access Method Parameter (AMP) in the // DD card is used to temporarily alter the buffer space requirements. There are two basic methods to perform this operation. The first is to use the BUFSP parameter to allocate a total amount of storage and let VSAM divide it up according to the processing requirements. This method requires that the user know the data and/or index CI size in order to be able to multiply the number of requested buffers by their respective sizes. One drawback to this technique lies in the possible alteration of the CI size at a later cluster definition. If this occurs, the user must ensure that the buffer space allocated in the JCL is recomputed. If this is not done, the buffer allocations may not satisfy the user's intentions. Another drawback is that VSAM is responsible for distributing the allocated buffer space and does so based on how the file is opened for processing. This may not always result in what the user wants. An example of this is when a file is opened for dynamic processing. The actual number of index buffers allocated may be less than what the user intended. Spanned record processing is another example.

A second alternative for reserving buffer space is to use the JCL DD card AMP subparameters BUFND for the data and BUFNI for the index. Through these parameters the user can specify the specific number of buffers required to process the dataset.

These parameters also give the user the flexibility of telling VSAM how to make the buffer distribution based on the type of processing to be performed in the program. This is very important whenever the user is processing dynamic files, which can have both direct and sequential processing. The user can determine the type of buffers required by knowing how the data is to be processed. This method of specifying buffer space is also superior to the use of BUFSP since it is not contingent on the data or index CI size. The number specified for each parameter indicates the number of buffers required. VSAM uses the current CI size to compute the buffer space needed.

JCL Specification for Buffer Space in DOS

There is only one method to allocate additional buffer space for a VSAM file in older versions of DOS through the JCL. This method is to use the BUFSP parameter of the // DLBL card. This is similar to the BUFSP in the // DD card. It is the user's responsibility to compute the correct buffer space requirements if this method is to be used.

This method is also sensitive to CI size changes. VSAM distributes the buffer space between the data and index (if required) buffers, depending on the processing options specified for the dataset at open time. The same drawbacks mentioned under the MVS // DD card apply to this DOS option.

A recent announcement to VSE/SP V4 has been the inclusion of the BUFNI and BUFND parameters to the // DLBL card. These parameters provide the VSE user with the same advantages described in MVS. The use of these parameters is recommended over the BUFSP. Users must convert to this new VSE/SP release to gain the advantages offered by these parameters.

Buffer Space Allocation Via the DEFINE ALTER Command

The user can alter the current buffer space for a dataset by running an IDCAMS ALTER command prior to processing the dataset. This operation has the same effect as using the BUFSP parameter on the JCL card. However, this operation takes longer and permanently alters the buffer space allocation. This extra step is not recommended because an ALTER has to be issued to prepare for different types of accesses.

BUFFER REQUIREMENTS FOR SEQUENTIAL PROCESSING

Sequential processing can be improved by providing additional data buffers. With three data buffers, VSAM improves performance by issuing I/O operations using CCW command chaining. However, there are not enough I/O areas to be able to perform I/O overlap with CPU processing. To achieve both command chaining and overlapping, the user would have to allocate approximately five or six buffers.

VSAM allocates data buffers starting on a page boundary. It is therefore possible to actually allocate additional buffers without having to allocate additional virtual or real storage to process the file. For example, a dataset with a CI size of 1K would have a minimum of two data buffers reserved. If the operating system being used was MVS, which allocates pages that are 4K in size, then the user could specify an additional two buffers without actually allocating any additional storage. This improves performance.

The user should be cautioned to the possible overallocation of VSAM buffers, which could have an overall effect on the program and system performance. If the user allocates many buffers, the possibility exists that the area could be paged out of storage before the user program can access the data for processing. This results in additional I/O operations being performed unnecessarily. The use of many buffers can also have an effect on system performance by reducing the number of real storage pages available for processing during the I/O operation. As mentioned in Chapter 2, it is better to increase the CI size to reduce the number of operations required to process the file and to maintain the number of buffers at a reasonable level.

Larger Data Buffers (CI Size) or More Buffers?

There have been many debates as to whether it is best to have a larger CI size specification or to use multiple buffers. Many benchmarks have been performed in this area. VSAM uses two techniques when reading and writing data to take advantage of any extra buffers that may be available to improve performance. With a minimum of three data buffers, VSAM performs CCW chaining. This has the net effect of reducing the number of execute channel program (EXCP) requests issued to the file. Multiple I/O areas are read/written with one EXCP. This can reduce CPU overhead and the total number of interrupts (SVC (Supervisor Call) and I/O) that must be issued for the dataset.

When additional buffers are provided, such as five or six, VSAM performs I/O processing overlap with program execution. In this manner, part of the buffers are made available for processing to the program while the remaining buffers are being used for an I/O operation. I/O operations occurring to the dataset are overlapped with program processing.

In general, it is best to increase the CI size to reduce the total number of EXCPs required to process the dataset. The CI size should not be made so exceptionally large that paging or virtual storage constraints are created. As mentioned earlier, a CI size of 4–8K is generally acceptable. With a minimum of three buffers, a user can obtain I/O chaining. If both I/O chaining and overlap processing is desired, a minimum of five buffers should be specified. Virtual and real storage availability are the major constraints affecting this decision.

Buffer Requirements for Direct Processing

For efficient processing of a direct file, the user would want to specify additional I/O buffers for the index. Since direct processing implies that each record read is completely independent of the previous one read, no read-ahead capability is possible. Therefore, additional data buffers would be wasted. Additional index buffer space should be allocated to at least accommodate all the high-level indices. Remember that index records are not read into storage until they are required for processing. The more index buffers that are provided, the less access to disk will be required to locate a record.

Information regarding the number of index levels and the number of records in the index can be found by using a LISTCAT of the cluster. This listing can also be used to determine the number of index set and sequence set records in the dataset. An excessive number of index buffers can have a negative effect on both the program and system. The effect is similar to that explained for the data buffers.

Buffer Selection for Spanned Record Support

As previously discussed, spanned records are logical records, which can be greater than the CI size. A spanned record can be smaller than one CI or as large as all the CIs in a CA. The minimum default buffering for spanned records is two data buffers. For KSDS files, one data buffer is kept in reserve for CI and CA splits. Therefore, if the spanned record occupies multiple CIs, multiple I/O operations would be required to read the spanned record through one buffer area. The spanned record would be assembled in a user-specified work area. For obvious reasons, spanned records cannot be processed in locate mode (i.e., the I/O area).

As can be observed,it is in the best interest of optimum performance to provide as many data buffers as possible up to the maximum spanned record size so that a record can be read in one I/O operation. This is one area where more data buffers is just as important as index buffers even when the file is being processed directly. One method would be to allocate enough buffer space in the cluster definition; however, if the dataset is opened for direct processing, index buffering will get preference. The best method is to use the BUFND parameter in the // DD JCL card. This parameter can be used to allocate a specific amount of data buffers for spanned records. Unfortunately this parameter is not available in the older versions of the DOS JCL. VSE/SP V4 provide his capability.

Effects of Excessive Buffer Space

The tuning of a VSAM dataset must be compared to the effect that this tuning will have on the rest of the jobs running in the system. Some tuning recommendations may suggest the allocation of sufficient data buffers to be able to read or write a complete CA into storage with one execute channel (EXCP) operation. This type of tuning could have a very positive effect on the performance of the dataset but could have other negative effects on the programs executing in the system.

If the CA size were set to a cylinder size, reading a full cylinder would take quite a few revolutions of the disk drive. During this time, the path (channel, control unit, and head of string) and device are busy. This effectively locks out any other requests that deal with datasets on the device and the path. Depending on the control units used, disk cabling and channel paths, other units may or not be available. I/O operations require that real storage be fixed (not moved) for the duration of the operation. When a large quantity of data must be read, a large number of real pages must be available for the duration of the I/O operation. As the program has read/written a large amount of data, affecting such a large amount of real storage, the user must ensure that these pages are not stolen before processing. If any page is stolen, additional I/O operations would be required to recover the data. All of these observations could have a negative effect on overall system performance. Another side effect is that a program that is processing this amount of data could become relatively process (CPU) bound. Therefore this could also affect any equal or lower priority jobs that are executing at the same time.

RECOMMENDATIONS FOR THE SELECTION OF I/O BUFFER SPACE

Any alteration of the buffer space requirements should be done for the duration of the program. It is best to let VSAM assume the default for the dataset at cluster definition. The amount of buffer space required should be supplied individually by program at JCL time. In the case of MVS, use the BUFND/BUFNI keywords in the AMP parameter of the // DD card. In the case of older versions of DOS, use the BUFSP parameter of the // DLBL card. In VSE/SP V4, use the BUFND/BUFNI keywords in the // DLBL card.

For sequential processing, it is best to specify more data buffers and use the default index buffer assumption. Index records are not read ahead, so one buffer will be sufficient for processing the file. The number of data buffers varies with the current workload; however, a specification of 5–7 buffers should be sufficient to achieve both processing overlap and CCW command chaining. In the case of direct processing, the number of index buffers should be increased to accommodate at least the number of index levels. Ideally, having the index set in storage would be good for processing. The number of data buffers required for direct processing should be defaulted to the VSAM assumption.

Dynamically processed datasets should have additional data and index buffers assigned because at any point the dataset could be processed in either fashion. The specification of BUFND/BUFNI is best suited for this type of processing, where the user can preselect the number of buffers desired for either type of processing based on the dataset's characteristics. This cannot be done in older versions of DOS, and the user must rely on a VSAM distribution at open time. An overallocation of space may be necessary to achieve the desired number of buffers. Use the BUFND/BUFNI parameters in VSE/SP V4.

Overallocation of VSAM buffers can have an overall negative affect on the system because of the excessive paging that may result. An additional exposure is that the data requested may be paged out before the VSAM user is ready to process it. This would require additional I/O operations to page the date back into storage for processing.

Chapter 7
SPACE ALLOCATION

A subtle tuning area lies in the allocation of DASD space to the VSAM dataset. This chapter focuses on certain VSAM options and parameters that can be used to define a dataset.

SPACE ALLOCATION OPTIONS

Several VSAM parameters are available to the user for defining the dataset. These options can be useful in improving the performance of the dataset. The options available are:

- Data space classification (CLASS) — DOS only
- SUBALLOCATION vs. NOALLOCATION — DOS only
- Multiple volume support:
  a. Volumes
  b. Ordered/Unordered
  c. Keyranges
- Total space requested

DATA SPACE CLASSIFICATION (CLASS)

This parameter is available to DOS users only. It gives the user some degree of control over the placement of the dataset in a suballocated environment. With this parameter, the user can classify the definition of suballocated space into different classes ranging from 0 through 7. In this manner, the user could assign a particular value to the space being defined and associate it with a particular catalog. Whenever that particular space is desired, the user could assign the definition of the cluster to the particular catalog that had control over that type of space.

This parameter was useful when DASD units had a certain amount of fixed head areas. The user could assign a particular class to represent the fixed head area and a different class to the moveable head area. Some of the common assignments were:

- CLASS (0) — Common usage area; is the default if no CLASS is specified.
- CLASS (1) — Fixed head area(s).
- CLASS (2-7)— User-defined area for other purposes.

The only major drawback to this type of classification is the possibility of increasing the total amount of VSAM space required due to fragmentation of the overall space allocated to VSAM. This parameter can be used whenever the user wants to allocate datasets together in a suballocated environment.

SUBALLOCATION VERSUS NOALLOCATION

This parameter is available to DOS users only. In general terms, when a cluster is defined, the user is required to define the amount of space desired for the file being defined. This is done through the use of the CYLINDERS, TRACKS, or RECORDS parameters for CKD DASD units and through the use of BLOCKS and RECORDS for the FBA DASD units (DOS only). The user then has the option of specifying whether the space is to be UNIQUE or SUBALLOCATED. If the space is to be unique, the dataset is to be the only one allocated within the space and has an entry in the VTOC. If the entry is to be suballocated, the space is taken out of a predefined area or pool and assigned to the user.

In the case of a suballocated file, there is no file label in the VTOC. In both of the preceding cases, the amount of space requested is immediately reserved for the cluster regardless of whether or not any records are loaded. With the NOALLOCATION parameter, the cluster can be defined into a suballocated space, but no space is reserved for the file until the file is opened for processing. With the use of NOALLOCATION and the REUSE parameters, the user can define dynamic datasets for use. Space is only occupied during the time the dataset is in use. This can be of importance when defining work areas such as compiler and sort work areas. This can have the effect of reducing the total amount of space required to support a DOS system. Remember that the use of the REUSE parameter limits the number of extents available to the dataset to 16 per volume.

Multiple Volume Support (KEYRANGES)

Several options are available to the user to handle requests that require more than one DASD volume. Whenever a user defines a dataset, a volume must be assigned to hold the defined cluster. The volume desired can be assigned using the VOLUMES parameter of the AMS DEFINE command. One or more volume serial numbers can be specified. The first volume specified becomes the primary volume, and the remainder specified become candidate volumes.

Note that there has to be enough space on the primary volume to accommodate the first primary allocation in up to five extents; otherwise, the allocation will fail. VSAM also tries to satisfy the future secondary allocations with up to five extents. The secondary allocation will fail if, after looking unsuccessfully for space on the current volume, VSAM finds that no additional candidate volume is available for allocation. Remember that when a candidate volume is used, a new primary allocation is made and not the secondary amount that caused the candidate volume to be used. This can lead to a large amount of wasted space on candidate volumes if care is not exercised. With the VOLUMES parameter, the user can exercise some control over dataset placement to balance device, control unit, and channel or subchannel utilization.

The search of the volumes specified in the VOLUMES parameter can be controlled by the use of the ORDERED parameter in the cluster definition. The ORDERED parameter can be used to instruct VSAM to follow the list of volumes as specified by the user in the VOLUMES parameter. If this parameter is not specified (default) or if UNORDERED is specified, the decision is coordinated with the MVS System Resource Manager (SRM), which will select the path with the least wait time. If the user wants a particular order to be followed, the ORDERED parameter must be specified.

One final option available to users who want to break down the access to a file is the KEYRANGES option. This specification can be particularly effective on very large files, although it can be applied to any file. Through the use of this parameter in combination with the VOLUMES and ORDERED parameters, the user can break down a dataset into separate extents on separate volumes while still maintaining the logical entity of the dataset. If sufficient "strings," which are logical access paths to the data, and buffers are available, having the dataset split among more than one volume could provide concurrent access to the dataset, which would improve performance. This is useful in an environment where the number of requests can be evenly distributed among the number of key ranges. In online environments that meet this criteria, performance can be improved, provided there is no additional interference on the selected volumes. To obtain this concurrent access, the index set records should be in storage; otherwise, access to the index that resides on disk will be single threaded.

Care must be taken when using the KEYRANGES parameter. The ranges specified must cover all key values in the dataset. If a key that is not included in any of the ranges is specified, the key is ignored and is not loaded into the file. Also, the number of volumes and key ranges specified do not have to match, although it is preferable that they do. If the number of key ranges exceeds the number of volumes, the excess number of key ranges will use the last volume specified.

Each new key range requires a primary allocation. Care must be exercised to ensure that the requested amount of space is the amount necessary; otherwise, excess allocation may occur in some key ranges and underallocation may occur in others. Secondary allocations for the key ranges may be made on the same or another volume.

Total Space Allocated

One area of concern is the amount of space allocated for the dataset. It is a good habit to do a LISTCAT of the dataset immediately after loading the dataset. An analysis of the Hi-Alloc-RBA and the Hi-Used-RBA will determine if the allocation requested is correct. The ratio of Hi-Used-RBA to Hi-Alloc-RBA should be approximately 90–95% unless a lower ratio is desired for future expansion. A 95% usage is a good figure since VSAM will allocate secondary space, if requested. Any excess space should be returned to the pool.

Another area to be examined is the number of extents allocated. If more than one extent is allocated when the dataset is loaded, it could be an indication of an underallocation, poor key compression, or disk space fragmentation. Although an immediate reorganization may not be required, the space allocation request should be changed. If disk fragmentation is indicated the volume should be analyzed. If necessary, datasets should be moved or space reclaimed from unused or expired datasets.

RECOMMENDATIONS FOR SPACE ALLOCATION

DOS users should use the concept of dynamic files as much as possible. This option is available through the use of the NOALLOCATION and REUSE parameters in the cluster definition. Disk space in a test environment can be reduced through the use of NOALLOCATION for test files. This could have a significant impact on the DASD space requirements for testing, especially when considering applications that may be in production. The CLASS parameter is not widely used and the number of DASD units available in the market that have the fixed head feature is vanishing. Other options available to the user for handling fast access, such as keeping the indices in storage, may be more practical.

The use of the KEYRANGES parameter may be very useful in the logical segmentation of a large file where concurrent access is desired. Note the following points before deciding to use the KEYRANGES parameter:

- The logical splits that are going to be used in breaking down the file should have activity evenly distributed to achieve optimum access.
- The volumes selected should have as little or no additional interference. Additional interference can affect access to that portion of the KEYRANGE dataset.
- The index for the file is kept in one physical area; therefore, other techniques such as defining additional storage index buffers to keep the high-level indices in storage should be used. Alternatives such as IMBED and REPLICATE are discussed in Chapter 8.
- Additional strings and buffers must be specified to provide concurrent access to a dataset. This takes up more virtual and real storage and may have an adverse effect on severely constrained systems.

One final tuning area for all datasets is to ensure that the dataset is not over- or underallocated in space. A review of the LISTCAT will be helpful in this analysis for correction.

Chapter 8
INDEX OPTIONS

Many KSDS files are processed directly in an online environment during the day and sequentially at night during batch processing. This chapter focuses on certain VSAM index options that can affect dataset performance when processed directly.

AVAILABLE INDEX OPTIONS

Several options in the definition of the indices are available to the user. The use of these options must be carefully weighed because some of the options sacrifice DASD space in return for faster data access. Some of these options are:

- REPLICATION of the index records
- Implanting the sequence set records within the data Control Areas (IMBED)
- Separating the index and data areas into different volumes
- Defining additional storage areas for the indices

The selection of any of the preceding options may involve the exchange of a highly available resource in exchange for a less available resource. The selection may depend on the abundance of a particular resource in your installation.

REPLICATION OF INDEX RECORDS

REPLICATION is the process by which the user informs VSAM that a separate track, or 62 FBA blocks, is to be assigned to each index record in the index extent. This may involve both the index and sequence set records. As a track is assigned to each record in the index, VSAM repeats the contents of the record as many times as it will fit within the track, or 62 FBA blocks. This has the effect of reducing the rotational delay involved in obtaining the index record. The sacrificed resource is DASD space, where one track per index record is given up. On the larger high-capacity DASD units such as the IBM 3380, this represents around 47K worth of space dedicated to one index record. The advantage is an average rotational gain of around 8.3ms per access. The amount saved could be higher on heavily used channels. This could be very significant in a direct access environment, where every data record accessed requires the reading of the indices from top to bottom. A selection of this option is an indication that the user has abundant DASD space but does not have sufficient virtual and/or real storage to accommodate the indices in storage. An additional disadvantage to replication involves the updating of indices. Since one full track is used for each index record, any time that the index record requires an update, such as after a control interval or area split, updating the full track will take longer than updating an individual record would have.

During the update of the indices, the VSAM file's integrity is exposed. Thus, when the indices are constantly being updated as a result of splits, replication may have a negative effect and the net gain on the average rotational delay may not be worth the investment or the exposure. The use of REPLICATE without IMBED is usually unwarranted since the price of IMBED is being paid by sacrificing one track per sequence set record without receiving the benefit of a faster access to the data through reduced arm movement. REPLICATE usually involves a specification of IMBED.

Sequence Set Records Implanted Within the Data Control Area (IMBED)

IMBED allows the user to have the sequence set entry corresponding to the Control Area (CA) written on the first track, or 62 FBA blocks, of the data CA. As a full track is assigned, the sequence set record is repeated the number of times that it will fit on the track. This type of option has the advantage of reducing the average rotational delay as with the REPLICATE option; and it could also reduce the arm motion because the sequence set record is imbedded within the data. Whether the arm is still in position between the reading of the sequence set and the reading of the data depends on the activity on the volume from other programs and/or systems. In a sequential processing, where the system follows the horizontal pointers in the sequence set to locate the next CA area to be processed, this type of option tends to keep the arm moving forward except for non-contiguous extents. This occurs because the arm does not have to go to the index area to obtain the next sequence set record and then come back to the next adjacent CA.

As with the REPLICATE option, the user has to be careful when specifying IMBED because an inordinate amount of space can be wasted if the CA definition is not equal to the maximum CA size available for the drive. For example, if the CA size were set to 2 tracks on an IBM 3380 DASD and IMBED is specified, the first track of the CA would be lost to the index. This means that 50% of the CA would go to the index and 50% to the data. This causes the dataset to take up much more DASD space and create more index entries, which could increase the number of index levels in the dataset. This could result in adverse performance, which would detract from the gains of using the IMBED option. It is imperative when using this option to ensure that the CA size equals the maximum CA size for the device being used. Also, IMBED should not be used for a file that is smaller than the maximum CA size. This was discussed in Chapter 5. In these cases, the user should make the primary and secondary space requests equal, forcing the CA size for the file to be set at its maximum value.

In this manner, only one index record, which is a sequence set record, is created. Since a minimum of one index buffer is allocated, this record will be held in storage, negating any visible improvements that could be gained by the IMBED option. The other disadvantage involves files that are constantly updating the index record as a result of control interval or control area splits. Each update to the index record requires that the entire track be rewritten, taking longer than an individual record update. The user must carefully weigh this in environments where additions and/or record expansions could cause splits to occur.

The use of the IMBED parameter is an indication that the user has abundant DASD space but does not have sufficient virtual and/or real storage available to accommodate the indices in storage. This parameter can be used without REPLICATE, but both should be specified together. In an era of high-capacity DASD units, we must take into consideration the probabilities of the access arm still being in position when the next request is issued to the dataset. In a high-activity system, the probabilities may be very low, negating the advantages of having the arm in position and requiring a direct access anyway. Each installation must judge its workload and its effect on IMBED.

Considerations When Using REPLICATE and IMBED Options

Several combinations are available to the user when using the REPLICATE and IMBED options. Figure 8.1 details the different combinations available to the user. Figure 8.2 summarizes the four options further.

Separation of Index and Data on Separate Volumes

This option is available to the user by simply specifying a different VOLUMES parameter when defining the DATA and INDEX portions of a cluster during the AMS DEFINE. For this option to be effective, the user should have available volumes that have

OPTION	DESCRIPTION	IMBED	REPLICATE
1.	Index and data separate	NO	NO
2.	Index (replicated) and data separate	NO	YES
3.	Index and data including sequence set	YES	NO
4.	Index (replicated) and data including sequence set	YES	YES

Figure 8.1. REPLICATE/IMBED combinations.

OPTION	COMMENTS
1.	This option requires the least DASD space. Since the index and data are separate, seek and search (rotation) times are the longest.
2.	Since each index entry occupies a separate track, or 62 FBA blocks, more space is required for the index. Seek times are the same as in option 1, but search time is reduced. Avoid this option because the price of replication is being paid for the sequence set, but not all the potential benefits are received
3	The sequence set records are removed from the index and combined with the data. The sequence set is replicated on the first track, or 62 FBA blocks, of the data CA. More DASD space is required for the file. Reduced access time for the sequence set is possible, depending on system workload and, in particular, the DASD volume(s) used. Seek and search times for the index set are as in option 1.
4	This option is a combination of options 2 and 3. Additional DASD space is required in exchange for reduced seek and search times. The actual effectiveness depends on the workload being processed.

Figure 8.2. Summary of REPLICATE/IMBED options.

little activity against them. This is not necessarily the case in installations that have high-capacity DASD units such as the 3380.

By separating the index from the data, the user can have two separate disk arms available to access the required information. This reduces arm contention. The actual effectiveness of this option depends on the additional external activity occurring in the rest of the system at the time that the file is being accessed. Also, on some of the older versions of DOS systems, the separation of the index and data placed a strain on the internal supervisory tables, which held temporary information that had to be restored at the end of the job. This table was called the Job Information Block (JIB) table. This problem has been resolved in the new versions of DOS.

Storing Index Records in Virtual Storage

The best performance option available to the user is to have the index records read into virtual storage and kept there. In this manner, access to the data would only involve the movement of the arm to the data portion, thus reducing the I/O operations required to access the record. To obtain these buffer areas, the user would have to indicate to the system the desired number of index buffers. This could be done through the BUFNI parameter in the // DD and // DLBL (VSE/SP V4) cards or through the BUFSP parameter in the // DLBL card (prior to VSE/SP V4). Sufficient virtual storage must be available to accommodate the requested buffers. Also, if the dataset has little activity, the page may be stolen for other operations, involving a potential page in I/O operation in these cases. This may affect performance because an extra I/O is performed; but it is the best alternative whenever sufficient virtual and real storage exists.

RECOMMENDATIONS FOR THE INDEX OPTIONS

Every option discussed is affected by the workload occurring in the system at the time the dataset is being processed. The user must evaluate which option or combination of options is best suited for the environment being analyzed. Wherever possible, keeping the indices in virtual storage is the best performance option as long as the extra index buffers do not cause virtual and/or real storage constraints. This option permits the user to maximize DASD storage resources. If virtual and/or real storage is a constraint, the use of IMBED and REPLICATE is a viable option. In this case, the user is optimizing storage at the expense of DASD space. If DASD and storage (real and virtual) are unavailable, do not use any of the options mentioned because they are going to aggravate the situation.

Chapter 9
CICS/VS CONSIDERATIONS

VSAM and CICS/VS are two common names when processing online. This chapter explores the major areas where VSAM can positively affect the online response time of a CICS/VS system.

CICS/VS AND VSAM

CICS/VS is considered to be the most widely used teleprocessing monitor in the world today. The system is designed to handle a large terminal network as well as many disk files. VSAM is the primary access method used by CICS/VS installations. CICS/VS supports all three VSAM organizations through a program called the File Control Program (FCP). User datasets are defined to CICS/VS through a table called the File Control Table (FCT). Through the different parameters supplied in this table, the user defines the type of access and options for the VSAM file.

This chapter addresses the topics of which a user tuning a CICS/VS system should be aware. Tuning a CICS/VS system is usually the product of a perceived problem. This perception can be reflected by symptoms such as:

- Short-on-Storage (SOS) conditions in CICS/VS.
- Slow or poor response times.
- Excessive paging activity.

- System statistics pointing to possible concerns such as many program compressions resulting in too many program reloads.
- Abends due to lack of storage or CPU time overruns.
- Overall availability and reliability problems.

One of the greatest constraints faced by CICS/VS users has to do with the lack of virtual storage on the system. This limitation is caused by being able to address only 16MB (24-bit addressing) of virtual storage. In the MVS area, many of the virtual storage problems have been contained or relieved through the use of MVS/XA, which provides users with the capability of addressing up to 2GB of virtual storage through the use of a 31-bit addressing scheme. This addressing scheme allows several areas used by CICS/VS to be moved above the 16MB line, thus releasing the areas it occupied below the 16MB line for other uses. The move above the 16MB line included the VSAM buffers pools. However, this move provides for only part of the relief required. CICS/VS R1.7, which has been available under MVS since December 1985, added some additional relief, such as a dynamic Terminal Control Table (TCT). Still, the majority of the CICS/VS control blocks must reside under the 16MB line. This is a result of some of the fields within the control blocks that use the high-order byte of an address to store bit type information. The MVS/370 user may still face the virtual storage constraint problem because of the 24-bit limitation.

The DOS user still has the 16MB addressing constraint but has received some relief with the announcement of the 128MB VSE/SP operating system. VSE/SP functions like MVS/370 with the concept of common or shared and private areas. The two major differences are:

1. VSE/SP is limited to nine regions, which is the VSE/SP term used to describe an MVS address space. This appears to be a marketing-oriented constraint and not a technical constraint.
2. The VSE region can be subdivided into multiple partitions to allow for multiprogramming within the region. The MVS address space is usually dedicated to one user who can do multitasking to accomplish almost the same task. The VSE user can also provide for multitasking within the partitions within each region.

However, the VSE/SP announcement does not necessarily resolve the virtual storage constraint problem for the large DOS CICS/VS user. This is so because the 16MB limitation still exists for the region, limiting the maximum size that could be allocated for a CICS/VS system. In the case of both MVS/370 and VSE/SP, the user could bypass the virtual storage constraint through the use of two CICS/VS features called Inter-Systems Communications (ISC) and Multi-Region Option (MRO). These features allow users to split their CICS/VS resources across two or more CICS/VS systems while still presenting a single image to the terminal user. These features do require additional resources and training before they can be used.

VSAM Considerations Under CICS/VS

The use of VSAM in an online environment can have both a positive and negative effect on the performance of the CICS/VS system. On the positive side, VSAM provides several parameters that, when used correctly, improve the performance of VSAM under CICS/VS. However, if these same parameters are used incorrectly, the net effect may be negative. Several factors affect the performance of VSAM in an online environment, which in turn can affect the overall performance of CICS/VS. The following areas are discussed in this chapter:

- The effect of allocating the proper number and types of buffers.
- The effect of allocating the required number of concurrent access paths or strings to the file.
- The effect of excessive buffer or string allocation on virtual storage availability.
- The effect of proper programming techniques.
- The effect of correct specification of file definition parameters to CICS/VS.
- The specification of OSCOR (MVS) and GETVIS (DOS) and its effect on CICS/VS.
- The effect of using Non-Shared Resources (NSR) or Local Shared Resources (LSR) on storage availability and processing efficiency.

ALLOCATION OF DATA AND INDEX BUFFERS

As discussed earlier, VSAM datasets to be used in the online environment are defined to CICS/VS in a table called the File Control Table (FCT). This table contains a series of parameters that are used to describe the file to CICS/VS. Note that the definition of VSAM datasets still has to be performed through the use of the AMS DEFINE command. The parameters supplied in the FCT contain additional information so that CICS/VS can process the file. Several parameters in the FCT are important to the performance of VSAM under CICS/VS.

The first parameters to be discussed are those related to the definition of the buffer or I/O areas required to process the file. As in the // DD card, the FCT can be used to define the number of buffers required for the index and data or the total amount of buffer space to be reserved for the file. These parameters are similar to the parameters that form part of the AMP (Access Method Parameter) parameter in the // DD JCL card. However, different from the // DD card, the parameters of BUFND and BUFNI are available to the DOS (VSE/SP) user through the FCT. This is the preferred method of telling CICS/VS how many of each buffer type are required to process the file. Another less preferred method is through the use of the BUFSP parameter. A change in the CI size of the file may cause the amount of storage requested for the file in the FCT to be inadequate. Also, providing CICS/VS with just a lump sum of bytes allows CICS/VS to decide how many of each type of buffer will be allocated. This does not take into consideration the user's knowledge of how that file is actually accessed and processed. For example, the specification of the 'BROWSE' subparameter in the SERVREQ parameter of the FCT is an indication to CICS/VS that the file will be processed sequentially at some point. Therefore, data buffers must be allocated to provide the read-ahead capability. However, this decision could be detrimental to the direct processing of the file since fewer index-level buffers will be allocated. This can be controlled if the user uses the BUFNI parameter to specify the actual number of index buffers required to process the file.

Selecting the proper number of index buffers for a VSAM file is important to that file's performance in an online environment. Ideally, the best alternative is to have all the indices in storage, thus avoiding having to read these indices from the disk drive. However, this may not be possible for large files. Therefore, as an option, the user should try to allocate enough buffer space to the index so as to be able to hold the index set records, plus one buffer for the sequence set to be processed. This reduces the number of index I/O operations required to access the record. If storage constraints do not permit the allocation of an index buffer for every index set record, then, at minimum, try to allocate sufficient index buffers that are equal to the number of index levels plus one. The number of index levels can be obtained from a LISTCAT.

If the dataset is to be used for sequential processing, the user should consider additional data buffers especially if the BROWSE facility is used. The BROWSE facility is a heavy user of software and hardware resources and can have a negative effect on the overall performance of an online system. The use of the standard BROWSE facility is not recommended and another technique is suggested in its place later on in this chapter. This extra allocation of data buffers should be monitored to control its impact on the total virtual storage requirements for the online system.

One of the greatest concerns that must be controlled in the definition of index and data buffers is the total amount of storage requirements generated. An excessive and unused capacity in this area can lead to a series of storage constraint problems such as Short on Storage (SOS) indications brought on by a reduced Dynamic Storage Area (DSA) caused by buffer overallocation or, in some cases, by abends caused by insufficient GETVIS or OSCOR. Even though VSAM buffers are defined above the 16MB line in MSV/XA, part of the control block structure still resides below the 16MB line. Lack of sufficient storage in the DSA can negatively affect CICS/VS system performance. The DSA is where CICS/VS allocates storage for the execution of a task, nonresident programs, I/O areas, and general work areas.

The CICS/VS statistics produced at the end of the day can be used to monitor the overall activity of a file in the online environment. The user should try to balance the number of buffers reserved for a file with the total I/O requests made during execution. A file that is used infrequently should not have more index/data buffers allocated than a file that has a significant amount of I/O activity. The CICS/VS statistics can also be used to identify the type of processing being done against the file. For example, a file that is being processed in a sequential fashion could have a browse count higher than its read total. Through the use of these statistics, the user could decide how to adjust the total number of buffers allocated to the dataset.

Unless there is a particular explainable reason, the number of buffers allocated to a file should be based on usage. Therefore, the files with greater activity should have more buffers allocated than those with less I/O activity.

Allocation of Multiple Access Paths or Strings

One of the most outstanding features that VSAM has over previous access methods is its ability to assign additional access paths to the file. These paths are called "strings." Using additional strings allows a user to have multiple requests to a particular file outstanding without having to wait for the previous I/O operation to complete. This allows concurrent access to the file by many tasks.

This capability is not without its price. The cost of using multiple strings involves the addition of virtual storage to contain the additional VSAM control blocks, and each string requires an additional index and data buffer. The FCT parameter used for specifying additional strings is called STRNO. The user can assign a value that indicates the number of concurrent accesses that are allowed for this file. CICS/VS handles its own string counts. This is done to keep VSAM from placing the entire CICS/VS partition into a wait whenever strings are not available or from dynamically allocating additional ones. In this manner, whenever the File Control Program (FCP) finds that no strings are available to handle the current request, the task is placed into a wait through the use of an internal CICS/VS Task Control Program (KCP) macro. The KCP in turn places the task in a wait state and searches the active task chain in order to dispatch the next available ready-to-run task. Only when none is ready to run will the KCP place the CICS/VS partition into a wait state.

The length of time that a string is held depends on the operation being performed. Certain operations hold the string for a relatively long period of time. Some of the operations that hold strings for a long time are:

- Get for update requests, which hold the string until the record is either updated, deleted, released through the UNLOCK command, or normal or abnormal termination of the task.
- BROWSE requests, which hold the string until the ENDBR command or normal or abnormal task termination.
- Locate mode reads, which hold the string until an UNLOCK is issued or the task terminates either normally or abnormally. (Macro Level).
- Mass inserts, which hold the string until the UNLOCK command is issued or a normal or abnormal task termination.
- Generic deletions, which hold the string until the request is complete or the task abnormally ends.

The preceding operations may require the user to specify more strings for the file than the default value, which is one. In general terms, the use of one string should be avoided because it can lead to VSAM file deadlocks. A deadlock occurs when a required resource is not available and will not be released as a result of another resource being unavailable. If the other resource is waiting for the original resource to free up, this condition normally never occurs, causing everyone depending on either resource to wait. This wait could be forever or until some action is taken to correct the situation. Two common lockouts are:

1. The "deadly embrace," which was just described. As an example, Task A wants to process Resource A with exclusive control. Task A obtains this resource. Meanwhile, Task B does the same thing, only with Resource B. Now Task A wants to obtain control of Resource B, which Task B currently controls. Upon requesting Resource B, Task A is placed into a wait, pending the availability of Resource B. Now Task B requests control over Resource A and is also placed into a wait because Task A still controls Resource A. Since both tasks are waiting for a resource currently held by each other, neither task is going to release the resource until it obtains the other resource. Therefore, both tasks are going to wait "forever."

2. A lockout caused by insufficient strings. For example, suppose a file has only one string assigned. If the user starts a BROWSE request, obtaining control of the only string, and in the middle of the browse, the user issues a read for update of a particular record within the same file, a lockout can occur. This occurs because the BROWSE command already has control of the only string. When the next read for update occurs, no more strings are available. The FCP places this task in a "wait" due to lack of strings. Since the task is never dispatched, it can never release the only string available.

As can be seen from the preceding discussion, too few strings can affect not only the performance of the file but can also cause lockouts, which may affect the overall performance of CICS/VS.

Selecting the number of strings required for a file depends a lot on the activity of the file. This parameter affects the number of data and index buffers required for processing the file. The minimum amount of index buffers must equal STRNO, whereas the minimum number of data buffers must equal STRNO plus 1. The more strings, the greater the amount of storage required to process the file.

The CICS/VS statistics that are normally printed at the end of the CICS/VS run can help the user keep track of how many times a file request has to wait for strings. Using the statistics of several days, a user can determine the number of strings required for each file. Just as important as increasing the number of strings available to a file is decreasing the number of unnecessary strings. This has the positive effect of reducing the required amount of storage and making it available for other requirements.

There is one final parameter that affects the number of strings available to a file. This parameter, usually left to default, is the STRNOG. This parameter is used to reserve a certain percentage of the number of strings rounded down for read-only inquiries. The default is 20%. This parameter can only be included in the FCT in an environment. If not all the requests for the file include read-only operations, there is a good possibility that there may be an unused resource if the number of strings specified exceeds five. In those cases, the user is urged to specify

STRNOG=0 so that all the strings specified are available for use. Although there is no parameter in the DOS FCT, the system also defaults to 20% in DOS.

Allocation of Buffer Space in a Multi-string Environment

The previous discussion regarding the allocation of data and index buffers did not take into account the definition of additional access paths or strings to the data. As each string constitutes a separate path to the data, the number of index buffers desired would have to be modified accordingly. The number of data buffers allocated must equal STRNO + 1. That is, at least one data and one index (if applicable) buffer per string are allocated. The additional or extra data buffer is allocated to handle CI/CA splits. Only one buffer is required for CI/CA split processing because an enqueue wait (CICS/VS FCP) is issued in order to protect the integrity of the dataset during this process. If a dataset receives many consecutive CI/CA splits, the user may get the impression that operating system waits are being issued when in fact these are only FCP waits until the split completes.

In the case of index buffers, the default is that the number of index buffers is equal to STRNO. If the user wants to have extra index buffers allocated so as to accommodate the number of index set records or index levels, an additional allocation using the FCT BUFNI parameter would be required. The formulas in this case are:

BUFNI = (# of strings) + (# of extra index buffers desired) (MVS)
BUFNI = (# of strings) + (# of index levels) (DOS)

Having sufficient index buffers allocated will allow the user to maintain the dataset's indices in virtual storage and thus reduce I/O operations. The number of index buffers requested would depend on the amount of virtual and real storage available to the user. Ideally the user would like to allocate sufficient index buffers to accommodate all index set records plus the numbers of strings plus 1.

BUFFER ALLOCATION OPTIONS

The buffer allocations mentioned thus far have implied that the areas reserved for a dataset for I/O operations (index and data) were for the exclusive use of that dataset. This is known as Non-Shared Resources, or NSR in VSAM processing. The other alternative available to the user is called Local Shared Resources, or LSR. Both of these buffer allocation techniques are available to the CICS/VS subscriber.

Non-Shared Resources (NSR)

Non-Shared Resources occur when the user defines the index and data buffers to be exclusively used by the dataset. This means that these areas can only be used by the dataset to which the areas were allocated. The advantage to NSR is that the buffers are dedicated and can be controlled by the dataset activity. However, note that the use of NSR is one of the largest contributors to the virtual storage constraint problem. Through CICS/VS R1.6.1 for MVS and R1.6.0 for DOS, the use of NSR was the default in the FCT for a VSAM file. The use of NSR is no longer the default in CICS/VS R1.7 and will require the reader to specify its use in the FCT. In releases prior to CICS/VS R1.7, the user had to avoid coding the SHARE subparameter in the SERVREQ parameter in the FCT definition so as to obtain NSR support for the file.

In CICS/VS R1.7, the user must code LSRPOOL=NO when defining the file in the FCT to obtain NSR support. If this parameter is omitted, the file definition defaults to Local Shared Resources pool number 1. NSR is best suited for datasets that have high activity. NSR is particularly best suited for:

- Datasets that have a lot of browsing activity because the read-ahead feature is activated through the use of chained I/O operations. However, because of the chained I/O, many data buffers may be used in the operation.
- Datasets that have a lot of CA split activity because VSAM uses chained I/O activity for formatting the affected CAs.

NSR also takes advantage of analyzing if the requested index set record is in its buffers before going out to issue a read on the index set record. This is called "look-aside buffer" hits. It will not look into the data buffers for the record nor the sequence set index buffer unless the same string is used.

The decision to use NSR lies in the availability of real and, more important in some cases, the availability of virtual storage. When deciding, the user must weigh the total I/O activity performed on the file throughout the processing day. These statistics are available at CICS/VS shutdown.

Local Shared Resources (LSR).

Local Shared Resources (LSR) allows the CICS/VS user to share resources with other datasets that are defined in the same region. This has the important effect of reducing the amount of virtual storage required to support the files. Some online files have low to medium access activity during the processing day. The I/O volume generated by these files may not justify the amount of storage space that must be reserved for their processing. Therefore, sharing resources makes sense for these files. As mentioned earlier, up to CICS/VS R1.6.1 for MVS and R1.6.0 in DOS, the user could specify LSR requirements by coding the SHARE subparameter in the SERVREQ parameter of the FCT. Only one subpool was available, and all files designated as LSR shared this storage subpool.

CICS/VS R1.7 was available for the DOS user in late 1987. Eight LSR subpools are available for MVS/XA users using the latest Data Facilities Program Product. These users can specify which of the eight pools is to be used for the dataset. This is done by using the LSRPOOL=n parameter in the FCT definition for the file. The value for "n" can be from 1 through 8. The default value is 1. Users of MVS/370 and DOS (VSE/SP) can only use LSR pool number 1.

LSR is a technique available to VSAM where the I/O buffers and strings allocated are to be shared among all the files participating in the LSR pool. If the DFHFCT TYPE=SHRCTL macro is not specified, CICS/VS scans each of the FCT entries looking for all the entries that had been flagged for sharing. During this scan, CICS/VS would determine the total number of strings and buffers for both data and index. It would also determine the maximum key size to be used by comparing each flagged file's key length until it found the largest key. One major problem with determining the size of the key up to CICS/VS R1.6.1 is that only available datasets were considered. If the dataset with the largest key was unavailable during this scan, the dataset could not be opened later. This problem was resolved by using the SHRCTL macro or by requesting that the dataset be opened initially. CICS/VS R1.7 finds the largest key regardless of the status of the dataset. The user could control the actual number of buffers and strings that are to be shared, depending on the specification made on the DFHFCT TYPE=SHRCTL macro. If this macro were omitted, CICS/VS defaults to 50% of the buffers and strings specified for all the files and computes the longest key required. The user can override the defaults by using the SHRCTL macro. In the majority of the cases prior to CICS/VS R1.7, the default value was used in many installations. With CICS/VS R1.7, the user should specify this macro to obtain better performance and additional buffers.

CICS/VS R1.7 offers several options to the user regarding the opening of files specified in the FCT. In all cases, files are not opened until after the CICS/VS initialization is complete. The user can request that the files be opened immediately after initialization by a special utility transaction and program or the file can be opened when the first request is made. This can be accomplished by specifying the OPENED or CLOSED and ENABLED or DISABLED keywords in the FCT for the file. The user can request that the file remain closed until explicitly opened by someone such as the Master Terminal operator. When the DFHFCT TYPE=SHRCTL macro is not used, the FCT is scanned to develop the appropriate LSR pool. During this scan, the STRNO parameter of each dataset associated with the pool assigned is used to determine the number of string and buffers to be allocated for the pool.

The maximum key length is also determined during this scan. Here, time is consumed to dynamically build the LSR pool. Also, the number of buffers allocated for the file will be based on the number of strings specified. If additional buffers or a faster allocation of the LSR pool is desired, the DFHFCT TYPE=SHRCTL macro should be coded. One of these macros should be specified per LSR pool to be used. In this manner, the user can request the number and sizes of buffers and the number of strings desired. The major drawback to this method of allocating LSR pools is that the user may have to adjust the specified SHRCTL figures whenever a file is added to or deleted from the FCT.

The size of the buffers reserved also merits comment. As discussed in Chapters 1 and 2, Control Intervals can vary in size from 512 bytes up to 32K bytes. Up to 8K, the sizes can range in increments of 512 bytes. After 8K, the sizes can range in increments of 2K. This means that 28 possible CI or buffer sizes are available. Shared resources only allocate certain buffer sizes. If a file uses a CI size that is not one of the selected ones, the next higher reserved buffer is used. The selected buffer sizes can be found in Figure 9.1. LSR uses a total of 11 buffer sizes.

BUFFER SIZE	BUFFER SIZE
.5K	16.0K
1.0K	20.0K
2.0K	24.0K
4.0K	28.0K
8.0K	32.0K
12.0K	

Figure 9.1. Valid shared buffer sizes.

Buffers are allocated for use by a dataset using the Least Recently Used (LRU) algorithm. It is easy to understand that when using shared resources, the sizes of the index and the data should be different to obtain the best results. If the index and the data were of different CI sizes, the LRU algorithm would create contention for buffer space only within each generic group, i.e., data or index. However, if the data and the index CI sizes were the same, there would be instances where the LRU buffer would be an index buffer and, as a result of having to read a data CI into storage, the index would be overlaid. Clearly, that is the last thing we would want. To obtain optimum performance, the index should remain in storage as much as possible to avoid having to reread the index, causing additional I/O operations.

A lot of the planning that went into using LSR through CICS/VS R1.6.1 or below went into ensuring that the data and index CI sizes never or rarely overlapped. This required a lot of time and patience. CICS/VS R1.7 under MVS/XA has provided some relief because the user can now separate the files into different subpools based on such characteristics as access and CI sizes to optimize LSR performance.

The user can obtain statistical information on how the LSR subpools are operating through the use of the CICS/VS statistics. The maximum number of strings and buffers that are available for use by a file is the number specified in the STRNO parameter for the file in the FCT. These parameters reflect the maximum available to the file even though a certain percentage of these specifications were actually allocated to the LSR pool. This could mean that a file using LSR might reflect being short on strings or buffers while the subpool may not reflect any exceptional conditions. To address this problem, the user could raise the numbers specified for the individual file in the FCT.

As mentioned earlier, for those users who have virtual storage constraint problems, LSR provides an excellent vehicle to alleviate some of the pressure. Files that are good candidates for LSR are those files with very low to medium volume that are processed mainly in direct mode. Also, files that have a low volume of browsing may benefit because the chained I/O feature is turned off, thus reducing the amount of I/O performed in certain cases. Files that do a lot of browsing will not experience as good a performance in an LSR environment because of the elimination of the chained I/O feature. Another type of file that may not perform as well when processed with LSR is a file that has a lot of CA splits because the elimination of the chained I/O feature could affect the overall effectiveness of the LSR pool by causing data buffers to be flushed out. Since CA splits cause a lot of data to be shifted from one area to another, the use of chained I/O would definitely be of use. Chained I/O can only be obtained using Non-Shared Resources (NSR).

LSR also provides "look-aside" buffer analysis. This "look-aside" occurs not only at the index level as in NSR, but also, in the data buffers.

OSCOR

Certain functions performed for CICS/VS require that a certain amount of storage be set aside for MVS Getmain/Freemain processing. Note that these types of Getmains and Freemains are different from the ones issued by the CICS/VS application and control programs that are handled out of the Dynamic Storage Area (DSA) by the Storage Control Program (SCP). An exception consists of requests for areas over the 16MB line for a CICS/VS running under MVS/XA. The SCP issues operating system Getmains and Freemains for areas above the 16MB line.

Operating system Getmains/Freemains are normally issued by the access methods used in CICS/VS, although at start up CICS/VS issues some Getmains and Freemains. After start up, CICS/VS does not normally issue any MVS Getmains or Freemains except for the formatted dump program (DFHFDP), which uses small control blocks of MVS storage to control the dumping of CICS/VS areas.

The normal manner in which one reserves area for the access methods use in CICS/VS is to specify an amount of storage in a Systems Initialization Table (SIT) parameter called "OSCOR". CICS/VS starts its initialization and proceeds to open all Open Initial files using the total available area set aside for the region (MVS) or partition size (VS1). Once this process is completed, CICS/VS will reserve an amount of storage equal to the OSCOR specified within the region/partition to be used by the access methods while CICS/VS is executing. The remaining area after the control/resident programs and CICS/VS tables are allocated, is the size of the Dynamic Storage Area.

In MVS, several storage areas are in the CICS/VS region. For example, there is free storage above the CICS/VS nucleus and below the MVS CSA. This area can contain free storage or other storage areas such as the LSQA, SWA, or SP229 acquired by MVS during job initialization. This free storage is not part of the OSCOR SIT request. CICS/VS usually sets aside the OSCOR below the CICS/VS nucleus that is usually adjacent to the DSA. It may not always be located in the same position due to the sequence of events that occurs when CICS/VS is initialized.

The use of the OSCOR parameter varies by user. For example, VSAM can use OSCOR for its buffers, whereas VTAM may use OSCOR for overflow requests from its processing. The important thing is that enough OSCOR has to be available or 80A or 40D abends can occur to CICS/VS. Files that are opened initially and closed after initialization release the storage back to the MVS free area to be used in later processing. Files that are opened after CICS/VS is initialized require OSCOR for their control blocks. Not only do the user VSAM datasets require OSCOR space to be opened if you open a dataset in a previously unopened catalog, but also VSAM requires OSCOR space to open the catalog.

One additional area that needs to be addressed is the topic of fragmentation. As storage is released back to the partition/region, it may not be in contiguous form. So the lack of a contiguous piece of storage can also cause problems for the CICS/VS partition/region.

CICS/VS R1.7 brings in a new concept of not opening the datasets until the file is first accessed. This means that all datasets will be opened after initialization. Thus some users are going to have to revise their OSCOR specification upward as a result of implementing R1.7. This does not mean that the region has to be made larger. The open initial datasets storage will not be used at this point, but will be allocated later. Analyze the requirements and monitor the OSCOR use when your CICS/VS system is operational. You should always leave room for normal expansion as new CICS/VS applications, terminals, and datasets are brought on line.

GETVIS

Two types of GETVIS storage are available in DOS/VSE or VSE/SP environment. The first type is known as the SYSTEM GETVIS area, a part of the SVA. This area is used by programs in the SVA to make them reentrant. It is used as a storage work area and can be temporary or permanent until the next IPL. The area can be used by CICS/VS control programs that would be placed in the SVA for processing. This area is used by DOS to place common routines used by many partitions, thus avoiding the duplication of a routine per partition. We could also place common user routines into this area, for example, Modulus 11 Routine. The second type of GETVIS is called the PARTITION GETVIS area. Each partition has a minimum of 48K bytes reserved for this area for each generated partition. It is automatically reserved by DOS when a job is executed. The size of this area is controlled by the size specified on the EXEC card. Thus the maximum size that can be specified would be the partition size minus the amount specified in the EXEC size parameter as long as the partition minimum is maintained. This GETVIS area is used by the access methods to store control blocks and I/O buffer areas. It can also be used to load routines for use by the programs executing in the partition. However, the main user of partition GETVIS storage in the CICS/VS partition is VSAM.

The allocation of GETVIS is of particular importance to the stability of the CICS/VS system. An excessive allocation to the GETVIS results in the generation of a smaller Dynamic Storage Area, which could result in excessive program compressions or, worse, short on storage (SOS) conditions. Both have a direct effect on CICS/VS performance and response time. A too-small allocation could result in a CICS/VS abend as a result of no more GETVIS storage availability. Both extremes are bad. Continuous monitoring and adjustment is recommended especially if the CICS/VS systems are in continuous expansion (e.g., new applications and data bases.).

One additional indirect concern of the GETVIS size is the extra partition storage required to support ICCF. Storage allocated to ICCF support also comes out of the partition size and can be quite large if it is not tuned. CICS/VS runs as a subtask of ICCF in the partition. The major concern faced by a DOS/VSE user is how large the CICS/VS partition can grow, especially if you are an ACF/VTAM user. The answer depends on many factors such as how large is the SVA, operating system nucleus, and how many additional partitions are required. The partition could vary between 8–11MB for a four-partition system (F1=POWER/VS, F2=CICS/VS, F3=ACF/VTAM, and BG=BATCH). The actual space left over for CICS/VS depends on the GETVIS size, the

CICS/VS control programs selected, and whether ICCF is being used. Many users initially believed that the 40MB available in VSE/SP would help solve this problem. In some cases it provided virtual storage relief but not for the large CICS/VS user. Many users have eliminated the use of ICCF by using third-party editors, which require less virtual storage. In many cases these software packages provide a quick relief to virtual storage constraints, providing improved function and performance at a slightly higher price. The only other solution is the use of MRO/ISC facilities. Even these facilities require additional virtual storage and CPU cycles in CICS/VS to implement.

PROGRAMMING TECHNIQUES

An applications programmer and/or analyst needs to be aware of several areas to avoid impacting VSAM and system performance. The following sections review some of the areas that should be analyzed:

- Browsing
- Protected Resources
- Updating
- Shareoptions

Browsing

Browsing is a technique available to online programmers that permits a file to be positioned at a particular record and then permits the programmer to issue sequential reads from that point on until a program determines the end of the search. This type of processing requires a lot of CICS/VS resources and has a tendency to monopolize a system. This is so because as long as the next record requested through the READNEXT command is in storage, the same task regains control. This prevents the task selection mechanism from dispatching another task, which may have a higher priority.

The runaway task indicator is reset. This, in effect, can lock out other tasks from executing and lead to CICS/VS lockouts due to programming loops caused by user errors. Thus many installations do not permit the use of standard CICS/VS browsing facilities. One commonly used method which limits the number of browses allowed at any one time in the system is through the use of the Class Maximum Tasks (CMXT) parameter.

CICS/VS provides another method to accomplish the equivalent of a browse without having to pay the resource price of a browse request. This can be accomplished by issuing a generic direct read to a particular key while specifying the greater than or equal option in the read. Once the first record is located, the user has the actual starting key value. If the user now adds a <u>one</u> to this key value and issues another read in the preceding format, the next sequential record will be obtained. As this was a direct read, the resources will only be used for the duration of the I/O operation. Other tasks can execute during the operation.

The adding of <u>one</u> to the key works for a numeric key. However, if the user has an alphanumeric key, another incrementing technique must be used. This can be accomplished by first testing whether or not the last digit has reached the maximum value. If not, do an assembler translate or COBOL transform to convert the low-order character to the next higher position in the collating sequence. That is, the letter "A" would be converted to the letter "B," the letter "C" would be converted to the letter "D," etc. If the highest collating value has been reached, the user has to reset the low-order character to the lowest collating sequence and the next-to-last digit must be analyzed in the same manner as the previous digit and so on. As can be seen, alphanumeric keys are slightly more complex using this method, but still the economies in system resources are well worth the effort.

One final area that should be analyzed is the stopping of the browse operation. Many programmers continue the browse until all the records meeting the browse criteria have been read. They do this even though there is not enough room to accommodate all of the data collected on the terminal screen. This technique adds additional resource requirements to the CICS/VS system to hold this temporary data; it also has a tendency to provide unequal response time to the user because of unpredictability of the number of records to be read and "hits" received. The user should only read the number of records that can be displayed on a terminal screen. A technique for saving the next key to be read and all generated screen pages for backward reference must be prepared by the user. This provides an opportunity for the requested information to be found before the end of the browse and before tying up additional resources. Also, this technique has a tendency to provide more consistent response times to the user because as soon as one page is available, the page is sent to the terminal.

Protected Resources

Protected resources is a means by which the user can provide data integrity to a VSAM file to correct an inadvertent update of a file when a task abends. This is also very useful in the synchronization of several updates that must occur on several files before the update is considered complete. Protected resources provides a means for CICS/VS to ensure that all updates are completed before completing the task. Should the task abend prior to the completion of a synchronization point, CICS/VS automatically reverses all updates performed by this task on protected datasets. Thus the file(s) would be restored to its (their) original state prior to being updated if the task abends. This action is called Dynamic Transaction Backout (DTB). The areas protected by DTB include record updates, deletions, and additions. To obtain protection for a file, the user must specify:

- DTB=YES for the transaction being executed in the DFHPCT TYPE=ENTRY. For CICS/VS R1.6.0 and later, DTB=YES is the default for the entire Program Control Table (PCT).
- LOG=YES for the file in the FCT definition.

There is a major difference as to how long the record and CI are held when using DTB versus not protecting the file. If a file is not DTB protected, the record and CI are made available to any other request upon:

- The completion of the REWRITE if an update is done, or
- The completion of an UNLOCK command to release exclusive control, or
- Task termination.

If DTB is being used, the record and CI are made available to any other request upon:

- Task termination (implicit SYNCPOINT), or
- An explicit SYNCPOINT is issued by the program.

CICS/VS uses a "window" called a logical unit of work (LUW) to determine which updates are still pending completion. This LUW is defined to begin when the task commences. Unless otherwise specified by the program, the LUW ends with the normal or abnormal task termination. This means that protected resources are being held until the end of the task, which could be a long time. This is the implicit definition of an LUW or synchronization point. CICS/VS provides the user with a means of defining different LUWs explicitly by issuing a SYNCPOINT command whenever the user has reached a point in the program where the updates can be considered valid, even if the program subsequently abends. This has the advantage of releasing the protected resources sooner for other users. As much as possible, the user should try to release any protected resources quickly by issuing a SYNCPOINT whenever logically possible.

Updating

An area that requires great care is that of updating an existing record. One of the initial tendencies is to write a program that reads a record, displays the necessary fields on the screen, and then issues a terminal read to await for the changes. This technique is not recommended because it holds the desired record and CI for the duration of the operator response. It also does not take into account any possible interruptions, which can cause the operator to delay entering the information for several minutes. The technique holds the record to ensure that the task has exclusive control of the record to be updated.

Many installations insist on pseudo-conversational tasks which will release any resources held. In these cases, the record is read and the pertinent data is displayed for update. The record is released as the task ends. A certain amount of information is saved so that the task can be restarted either in the communications area or temporary storage. When the data is received from the terminal, it is edited and, if correct, the record is reread with exclusive control to update the record. In this manner, the record to be updated and the Control Interval are only held for the duration of the update. Any operator interruptions do not affect the length of time that the record and CI are held.

SHAREOPTIONS

SHAREOPTIONS is a parameter that can be indicated during the creation of a cluster that specifies the type of dataset sharing options that are going to be in effect for the file. The purpose is similar to the use of the DISP= parameter available to the user in the JCL DD or DLBL card. However, the SHAREOPTIONS parameter is given at cluster creation and can include a parameter to specify cross-system usage (not available in DOS). It is also used to specify cross-region sharing. Generally SHAREOPTIONS 1 and 2 normally do not affect performance as much as data integrity, although multiple accesses are permitted and can cause performance problems. SHAREOPTIONS 3 allows the dataset to be opened for output by multiple users. The only effect on performance (in addition to the concern for data integrity) would be the interference caused by two or more programs accessing the same dataset. This interference can affect online response if an online program has to compete for resources with a batch application. Batch applications have a tendency of gaining control of the disk unit and head of string more often than the online system because the dataset is usually processed sequentially. Special care should be taken to reduce this interference, especially if the dataset is still being accessed by the online program.

Of particular importance in relation to performance is the specification of SHAREOPTIONS 4 for the dataset. This specification automatically forces a read of both the data and index CIs for each record, even if the record is already in memory. This type of specification nullifies any index buffering that may be done by the user. Never use SHAREOPTIONS 4 for datasets defined in LSR. The effect of this SHAREOPTIONS specification can be felt in both an online and batch program. Therefore, the selection of

SHAREOPTIONS and implementation should be carefully analyzed by the user prior to its selection.

The SHAREOPTIONS parameter should be specified at the CLUSTER level to ensure that the data and index receive the same specification. If specified at the data level, the index level will default, and vice versa, which could lead to problems as the default may not be what was desired.

GENERAL FILE CONSIDERATIONS

One minor area that should be considered whenever many VSAM datasets are being used in CICS/VS is the number of secondary allocations used by each dataset. Secondary allocations require more virtual storage to maintain track of them. Therefore, reduce the number of secondary allocations on all datasets to a minimum by reorganizing datasets with multiple extents. VSAM tries to allocate the requested space contiguously. However, if a contiguous space is not available, the allocation may be satisfied with up to five extents.

This applies to both the primary and secondary allocation requests. If more than one extent is needed to satisfy the requested quantity, the number of extents used reduces the total number of available extents (e.g., 123 MAX) for the dataset. This can become a problem in datasets that have reached the maximum expansion and receive insertions online. If no more extents are available when a Control Area split occurs, an error will occur, causing the loss of the data until the file is reorganized.

Test CICS/VS Systems

One area that is usually overlooked when tuning a system is the test CICS/VS region, or partition. In too many cases, the test partition is an exact copy of the production CICS/VS system, which tends to create unnecessary constraints in the test system, possibly affecting overall systems performance. For example, there is no need to have all the strings, data, and index buffers specified for all the datasets in the FCT in a test system as in the production system. Normally, testing of an online program does not generate the volume that the production system would. In fact, having very few strings (i.e., one string) could force the detection of program and design errors that hold the string indefinitely. This type of bug would be harder to detect in a production system because other strings would be available for processing.

Since many of the datasets in the test FCT reflect files that are already in production, there is no need to have these files opened initially at CICS/VS startup. This causes CICS/VS to take longer to initialize (CICS/VS R1.6 or below). Many test files could be smaller extracts than the production datasets, thus reducing DASD requirements. In fact, many installations keep test files on tape and load them only when testing is required.

RECOMMENDATIONS FOR VSAM UNDER CICS/VS

The use of Local Shared Resources appears to be the direction that is being taken with CICS/VS. This is evidenced by the enhancements made to VSAM processing in R1.7. Further enhancements in this area can be expected. Low and medium activity datasets are perfect candidates for LSR processing. LSR can be used for high-activity datasets in MVS/XA since these datasets can be assigned to their own subpool. The use of the SHRCTL option is highly recommended because additional data/index buffers can be allocated. The default number of strings is usually sufficient. The use of the SRHCTL macro with all parameters specified increases the speed of creating the LSR pool.

From a programming point of view, the user is advised to limit or eliminate the use of the CICS/VS browse facility. If the browse facility cannot be eliminated through the use of a direct read, it is strongly suggested that the user limit the number of concurrent browses through the use of CMXT parameter in the DFHSIT and the use of the TCLASS parameter in the DFHPCT TYPE=ENTRY parameters. Other good programming techniques include the proper use of protected resources, including the use of the SYNCPOINT macro, proper update practices, and the limitation of the SHAREOPTIONS 4 parameter for the dataset.

Chapter 10
MISCELLANEOUS CONSIDERATIONS

This chapter reviews certain areas that can affect VSAM performance but do not warrant separate chapters for each topic. Each of the individual topics in this chapter can contribute to good VSAM performance.

RECOVERY VERSUS SPEED

Whenever a VSAM dataset is being loaded for the first time, the user has the option of specifying the RECOVERY parameter. Through the use of this parameter, the user can restart from the last CI written should an abend occur during the loading of the dataset. The specification of RECOVERY instructs VSAM to preformat the Control Area to the software end-of-file (SEOF) indicators.

If an error occurs during the load, the location of the last end-of-file indicator can be found and the load restarted from this point forward. The only problem with this logic is that the user must code the restart routine. A VERIFY will not locate the end of the dataset because the High-Used-RBA is not updated when the load program cancels. Most users do not have a recovery routine coded. Therefore, the additional formatting of the CAs creates an unnecessary overhead that can be eliminated to improve load times. Unfortunately RECOVERY is the default option when defining the cluster. The user is forced to specify the SPEED parameter to instruct VSAM not to preformat the CAs. Once the dataset is loaded, the recovery option is set to "on."

Index processing is always in recovery mode, and the SPEED option is not valid at the index level.

ERASE versus NOERASE

The user has the option of asking VSAM to clear to binary zeros any area used by a dataset whenever the dataset is deleted. This operation can take a significant amount of time whenever a large dataset is involved. Unless the dataset contains highly classified information, it is recommended that the user specify NOERASE for the dataset to reduce the amount of time required to delete the dataset. On removable DASD media, the dataset that has ERASE specified requires that the dataset be mounted online for the delete operation to complete. The user can override the ERASE option in the DELETE command. NOERASE is the default. If the information is so sensitive, the user is urged to protect this data area using a security package rather than the ERASE option.

Dataset Fragmentation

Dataset allocations for either the primary or secondary space that take more than one extent to satisfy are an indication that the space left on the volume is either insufficient or that it is highly fragmented. This is a clear indication that a planned restructure of the datasets on the volume is required. An initial analysis of datasets that contain a large number of CI and CA splits should be done, especially if these datasets also contain secondary allocations (multiple extents). As CI/CA splits can result in large unusable spaces to be allocated, these datasets should be reorganized first. In this manner, any unused space can be recovered and reorganization of the volume avoided.

This planned restructure should include the analysis of the space requirements and allocations requested for all the files on the volume. Unused space should be immediately returned to the volume for future use. If space is not found, the user should plan to move some of the datasets off the volume onto another so as to defer any future space allocation problems. As a final alternative, the user should plan to back up all the datasets on the volume to tape and plan to reload every dataset through the use of AMS DELETE and DEFINE commands. This whole operation can take time and will require good planning to avoid any operational problems.

Multiple Extent Datasets

Datasets with multiple extents are also an indication of fragmentation or poor primary/secondary allocation requests. These additional extents take up additional space in virtual storage and usually represent additional open overhead in processing the dataset. Secondary allocations are a good way of recognizing when a dataset needs to be reorganized. This is especially true when the extra allocations are a result of CA splits. Since CA splits move around half of the data in a CA, large amounts of unusable free space, as well as misused DASD space can result.

Multiple extents can also indicate poor key compression whenever these extents occur immediately after a load of a dataset. A new calculation should be made to ensure that VSAM is performing proper key compression. This condition is not readily identifiable and may require the listing of the index records to analyze if the condition exists. When reviewing a sequence set index record, the user should look at the area past the initial control information located at the beginning of the index record which has a displacement of X'18'. VSAM places the free CIs by relative number starting at this point in descending order. If the number of free CIs exceeds the FREESPACE percentage requested, there is a potential loss of data CIs in the CA. An analysis of several sequence set index records should be performed to determine the actual extent of the key compression.

Multiple extents may result from a user plan. For example, let's take a dataset that spans one-and-a-half 3350 DASD volumes. If the user requests an allocation of CYLINDERS (554 277), the dataset will actually occupy two full volumes. This is precipitated by allocations for space on a new volume, which cause VSAM to allocate the primary quantity. As a result, the dataset is overallocated by half a volume. To get the appropriate allocation, the user would have to specify CYLINDERS (277 277), causing VSAM to allocate two extents of 277 cylinders on the first volume and one extent of 277 cylinders on the second volume when the dataset is first loaded. These extra extents were planned to allocate the correct DASD space to the dataset.

Secondary Allocation Specification

As mentioned earlier, the user should always specify the secondary allocation for a dataset, especially if the dataset is a KSDS file to avoid unnecessary problems when extensions are required. Just as important is the amount of secondary space selected. This amount should be large enough to avoid continuous secondary allocations during an execution of a program, yet small enough so as not to cause overallocation of the file nor cause space allocation problems due to lack of space on the DASD units. Each time additional space is required, VSAM goes through an "open" type processing which takes time. Proper specification of this value can reduce unnecessary handling time and possible cancellations.

VSAM ISAM Interface Program (IIP)

The VSAM IIP was an emulation routine provided to ease the transition from an ISAM into a VSAM environment. All that was required was the use of the IDCAMS REPRO and DEFINE CLUSTER facilities to convert ISAM datasets to VSAM. Program modification or compilation was not required to obtain the benefits of having a VSAM dataset. The JCL has to be altered to reflect a VSAM dataset. When the dataset is opened as an ISAM file, a routine will intercept the ISAM open and convert it into a VSAM open. The appropriate pointers are established so that any I/O for the dataset will be handled by the VSAM IIP. Users have found that IIP is an easy way of converting to VSAM.

There is a general tendency to believe that the IIP, being an emulation program, creates an overhead whenever processing the dataset. The IIP in actuality takes up fewer CPU resources than if the dataset were converted to native VSAM since the IIP is limited toward emulating the ISAM process and, therefore, does not have to have all the additional processing required for the full VSAM support. Unless there is a particular feature desired in the VSAM process such as the immediate recovery of space available through the DELETE command, there is no need to rush the conversion of IIP programs to native VSAM.

Index Splits and Multiple Extents

Index splits and multiple extents can occur for any KSDS file. Normally space is requested for the data portion of the dataset and, based on this request, VSAM allocates enough space to cover the index area. However, there are some occasions where the user may misjudge the amount of space required, causing VSAM to also misjudge the amount of index space required for the dataset. As a result, additional space is needed not only for the data portion, but also for the index. This causes additional overhead processing and may result in an index being split in different areas of the DASD unit, resulting in additional seeks in the index area, which affects performance.

Index splits can occur in a volatile file that receives insertions and has a poor key compression algorithm. As a result of the split, the new index record is written out at the end of the index area, thus causing additional seeks when processing the dataset, especially if an additional extent has been added to the index area.

The preceding situations do not occur frequently and can be spotted using an IDCAMS LISTCAT. Datasets that have any of these conditions should be reorganized whenever possible.

WRITECHECK

WRITECHECK is an available feature that requests that VSAM provide the necessary CCWs in the channel program to reread any CI that has been written. The purpose of this request is to verify that the data just written are correct and that no errors occurred. Tape units have an additional read head following the normal read/write head mechanism to perform the reread operation automatically in the same pass. DASD units only have one read/write mechanism. Therefore, to verify that the data were written correctly, the DASD unit must wait for a full revolution of the disk before the data returns under the read mechanism to be reread for verification. This process elongates any DASD operation that involves a write operation, making the operation at least one DASD revolution longer. DASD technology has advanced tremendously since disks were introduced in the early 1960s, making the write check or verify option unnecessary. As this option makes the whole operation last longer, it is highly recommended that this option not be used, especially in an online environment where response is critical. In the verify operation, the data are not actually reread into the computer storage. To read it back into storage, a separate I/O area would be required or the original data would be destroyed in case a real error is found. Having a separate area would increase storage requirements and would also entail comparing the two areas, the original and the verify area. Instead, the verify operation involves the rereading of the data with a CCW that has the skip bit CCW FLAG turned on. This indicates to the control unit and channel that the data are not to be read into storage but discarded instead. However, as the data are reread, the cyclic checks or error correction code (ECC) are re-created and verified, ensuring that the data are valid. If an error occurs, the original data still in storage are used to rewrite the data to try and correct the error.

The use of the WRITECHECK feature should be limited to those datasets that need a high degree of accuracy because the data cannot be re-created. As many of the problems associated with data destruction have nothing to do with the actual data being written (for example, head crashes or an operator/program error that overlays datasets), it is probably better to have the data written twice on separate volumes. Called a "mirror" file, this mirror dataset can be used to recover from catastrophic errors. This is a better solution because the writes can be spread across separate paths without as much degradation to the response time.

Back Up

Several methods are available to the user to back up the VSAM datasets, including several excellent third-party software products. A full discussion of these products is beyond the scope of this book. However, a discussion of the IDCAMS REPRO/

EXPORT/IMPORT facilities is appropriate. The REPRO facility is widely used to back up and restore data files. For best results with the REPRO facility, be sure to use a large block size for the tape file being used for backup (e.g., one close to 32K bytes) because a regular Sequential Access Method is used, which may have limited buffering facilities. The VSAM dataset should be given as many data buffers as can be spared without overtaxing the system. Approximately 6–10 data buffers would probably be sufficient for improved performance. The EXPORT/IMPORT facilities will also benefit from the additional buffering and tape output block size. The main difference between the two methods is that in the EXPORT/IMPORT process, a definition of the cluster is included in the backup process. This means that the dataset can actually be removed from the catalog without having to delete the cluster.

However, if the user plans to alter the cluster definition, the use of EXPORT/IMPORT should be reevaluated because the altering of some of the cluster definitions involves the deletion and redefinition of the dataset. ALTER cannot be used to change the CI size.

Both the preceding alternatives have a lot of overhead associated with them. As a result, many installations have written their own programs to provide the backup capability while at the same time producing a report as a by-product. This has the advantage of adding more buffers to the VSAM dataset. If the user has a program that is already reading the entire dataset, this program could be altered to produce the output backup tape at a reduced cost because the data is already read. For example, some installations prepare the backup as a by-product of the update run.

Contention

One of the biggest areas that affect performance is the area of channel, control unit, head of string, and disk unit contention. Generally the balancing of channel and disk units is external to the topics discussed in this book. However, it is important to avoid running batch jobs against disk units that are being used online. You should especially avoid running backups on units being used by the online systems. Multiple paths to the datasets are just as important to provide alternate paths to the data. Spreading the datasets used in an application across several volumes and paths can be a positive performance enhancer.

Hardware

An area that is generally not addressed is the hardware configuration. A study of how the system is generated (IOCP generation for large machines) and how the DASD control units and channel paths are connected can give some ideas as to which units have a better hardware balance. Normally this task is performed by the systems programmers who may also be assigned to the VSAM tuning function. In some cases, the DASD administrator may be responsible. A review of the hardware will help you see the overall picture.

Switching DASD Units

VSAM provides a certain amount of hardware transparency to the user. However, different DASD units require a review of the space allocation requests for the dataset. For example, if a dataset residing on a 3350 DASD unit had an allocation of CYLINDERS (100 10) and were to be moved to a 3380 DASD unit without any change in the requested amount, a significant increase in DASD space would result on the 3380. This is particularly true when determining the CI and CA sizes, especially for those datasets allocated in tracks and/or records. The switch to and from FBA and CKD units also requires planning and care. In general terms, switching DASD units is not as transparent from a performance point of view.

VSAM ALTERNATE INDEX FACILITY

Alternate indices provide the user with a means of accessing a dataset by a different key from that used to load the dataset. An example is a payroll file loaded with an employee number as the primary key. If the user needed to access this file using a social security number, an alternate key could be selected, meaning that the reader could use either of the keys to obtain access to the same record. This facility is available in VSAM and can enhance the usability of the dataset by reducing the number of sorts required to handle the dataset as well as reducing the duplicity of data sorted under different keys.

Note that alternate indices are a functional enhancement and not a performance enhancement. The major advantage of using alternate indices is that the program provides only an access key to obtain the record through the alternate index. Alternate indices is not a new concept. In the past, this function was provided by having a separate dataset that contained the alternate keys with the respective primary key equivalence. The user would issue a read employing the alternate key dataset to read the desired "index" record, which contained the address or primary key of the desired record. The user would then issue a read to the main dataset employing the new key value to locate the desired record. In general, the programmer had to program two I/O operations to obtain the desired record through an alternate key file. Changes to a base dataset that involved additions and/or deletions would require the programmer to issue a second I/O operation to the alternate file to add and/or delete the alternate key record.

In some cases, the desired alternate key would have "duplicates" such as using the employee name as an alternate key. Tie breakers are made by either appending a sequential key number or the original primary key to the end of the alternate key. To read the alternate key where duplicates exist, a generic read is issued to locate all the records that begin with the same alternate key.

VSAM provides a means where the program need not issue two I/O operations to obtain the desired record in the main file. The main file is called the "base cluster." VSAM optionally can be requested to automatically handle additions and/or deletions to the base cluster to be reflected in the alternate index datasets. VSAM can also be informed that there will be duplicate keys. The major enhancement over past processing is that VSAM can be made to automatically build the alternate indices over the base cluster and to maintain synchronization between the alternate indices and the base cluster, which requires the programmer to issue only one I/O operation in the program to obtain the desired record. Unfortunately there is a price to pay. For this added enhancement, the amount of overhead is quite extensive, to the point that there are third-party software enhancers to this alternate index process. It is more efficient to handle the alternate indices independently, as in the past, by creating separate alternate index datasets and issuing individual I/O requests to each file. This is in spite of the ease of use that VSAM provides. Also, good buffering can be provided individually for each dataset.

Buffering Alternate Indices under CICS/VS

Most of the time it is best to let the BUFFERSPACE parameter default to the VSAM CLUSTER DEFINE default. However, whenever the base cluster is being accessed through the alternate index, the buffer allocations provided at JCL time apply to the PATH that defines which alternate key is being associated with the base cluster. To obtain more than the default amount of BUFFERSPACE for the base cluster, the user must perform one of two options. The first option is to define the desired BUFFERSPACE during the definition of the cluster. The second option is to use the IDCAMS ALTER command to alter the dataset's BUFFERSPACE prior to use.

Automatic Versus "Do It Yourself"

The decision must be made as to which is more important, ease of programming or performance. Both have valid trade-offs, which must be evaluated in the user's environment. From many people's point of view, the best way to improve VSAM's alternate index performance is to not use it.

VSAM THIRD PARTY SOFTWARE

Several excellent packages are available in the software market that enhance VSAM performance and make tuning easier. It is our experience, however, that these tools need to be given to someone who is familiar with VSAM and has been involved in some type of tuning activity, preferably VSAM. There are several reasons for this recommendation. First, these packages usually make recommendations based on a series of assumptions. The recommendations developed are just that — recommendations. Unfortunately too many people take these as "gospel" without giving any further thought to their environment. A basic understanding of VSAM is important for anyone using these packages. Second, the tuning of VSAM datasets cannot be separated from other related items. Many of these packages are not aware of how the dataset is used nor of how it relates to other datasets. In addition, external factors such as real and virtual storage constraints are not considered by these packages when evaluating datasets. In summary, these software products are tools and do not eliminate the need for training and just plain old reading.

RECOMMENDATIONS.

The preceding recommendations should be used as appropriate. Although these recommendations are classified as "miscellaneous," their correct use can have a positive effect on dataset performance. This is especially true if the dataset is large.

Chapter 11
SUMMARY OF THE VSAM TUNING PROCESS

This chapter serves as a summary for the entire book. Specific tuning areas are identified along with referals to the appropriate chapter to review. In particular, this chapter helps you identify "Where do I start to tune VSAM?"

WHERE DO YOU START?

Tuning is a continuous process that requires constant user attention. Before starting to tune the VSAM datasets, you must establish why the datasets are going to be tuned. In addition, the datasets to be tuned have to be identified. The datasets to be initially selected should meet one or more of the following criteria:

- The datasets should be representative of the workload being performed on the system. These datasets should be used daily or be online.
- The datasets should consume resources. These resources could be in the form of run processing times or DASD space, or they could form part of a "critical window" that must be met.
- The dataset does not necessarily consume resources, but it requires a quick access for a fast response. This can be seen in an online application.

The important aspect is that the datasets selected represent an important part of the installation's workload. A LISTCAT of the selected datasets would be the best starting point. Appendix A provides a guide of the more important fields to be considered in this evaluation. Also important in this decision is the determination of the critical resources. A definition of which resources are scarce and which ones are abundant will be useful in the tuning process.

Starting the Tuning Process

Using the LISTCAT, divide the datasets into two categories. One category is those datasets needing immediate attention, and the other category is those datasets that are not as serious. Use the following guidelines to separate the datasets into these two groups:

- Does the dataset take a long time to process?
- Does the dataset reflect many CA splits?
- Does the dataset receive online insertions?
- Is the dataset accessed online frequently?
- Is the dataset excessively overallocated?

A "yes" answer to any of the preceding questions would place the dataset into the first category. The datasets in this category should be tuned first. The remainder of the datasets should be placed in the next category for later tuning. Some of the guidelines that can be used for the second category are:

- Are there many CI splits on the dataset?
- Are backup and restore times critical because of a "critical window"?
- Does the dataset have some undesired specification such as IMBED, REPLICATE, RECOVERY, SHAREOPTIONS 4, or ERASE?
- Does the dataset have an overallocation of FREESPACE? Should the dataset have a specification for FREESPACE due to insertions or lengthening of records?

- Does the file have multiple extents because it has not been reorganized over a long period? Is the limit on extensions about to be reached?

Some of these questions can be moved between categories, depending on the critical resources defined for your environment. In other words, feel free to set up your own guidelines.

One final recommendation when tuning datasets. Try to schedule the changes and spread these changes across several weeks, if possible. Too many changes can cause unnecessary problems. Proper testing procedures should be in place not only to make the changes but to measure the results after the changes. This is particularly important for online datasets. The following topics discuss the different questions presented.

LENGTH OF PROCESSING TIME

Several factors may affect the length of time required to process a dataset. One of the first areas to be considered is somewhat external to VSAM tuning. This deals with proper load balancing of the DASD units and channels. This type of tuning will be done by the installation system programmer, which in many cases may be you. Unfortunately, high-capacity DASD units will contribute to this situation.

Many installations have found that these units cannot be allocated more than 60–75% in order to have control over device and channel utilizations. MVS/XA has improved this situation some so that channel utilizations can be higher. One way of improving this situation is to spread the datasets across several devices and paths to minimize the contention problem but may require better controls in order to ensure synchronized backups of all application datasets.

From a dataset point of view, slow processing may be due to several factors. The CI size selected can be an important performance reason for slow processing if the dataset is being read sequentially. Larger CI sizes provide better performance because of the reduced overhead times. Another area that can have a positive impact on the dataset's performance is the buffering provided. For sequential processing, the more data buffers provided, the more chaining and overlapping are performed. For direct processing, more index buffers will improve access to the records. You should also verify that an excessive amount of buffers is not causing the slow processing. Too many buffers require additional virtual and real storage. If the data is processed in a highly active system, the buffer may be paged out of real storage and require an additional I/O operation to bring it back into storage. This has an adverse effect on performance.

You should also review the amount of FREESPACE allocated to the dataset. An overallocation of free space causes the dataset to be larger and requires more I/O operations to process sequentially. Free space could have been caused by CI and CA splits. If this is the case, you should analyze the amount of FREE SPACE to ensure that it is set correctly. CI/CA splits take time and can make processing slower, especially if IMBED and/or REPLICATE is specified.

If the dataset is a KSDS, you should analyze the CA size. A poor CA size selection can increase the number of index levels in a dataset which negatively affects direct processing. If the CA size is combined with other options such as IMBED, more space is required, making processing slower.

Finally, you should verify if SHAREOPTIONS 4 has been specified for the dataset. If it has, it could be a reason for the slow processing. Ensure that this specification is really required.

For additional information, review the following chapters:

- Chapter 2, Control Interval Size
- Chapter 3, Free Space
- Chapter 4, CI/CA Splits
- Chapter 5, CA Size
- Chapter 6, I/O Buffer Allocation
- Chapter 8, Index Options
- Chapter 10, Miscellaneous Considerations

CA Splits

CA splits can be very costly, especially in an online environment. When a dataset reflects many CA splits, the dataset should be analyzed to ensure that the proper FREESPACE has been allocated. The frequency of dataset reorganization should also be evaluated. FREESPACE and dataset reorganization go hand in hand.

For additional information, review the following chapters:

- Chapter 3, Free space
- Chapter 4, CI/CA Splits
- Appendix A, Reading an IDCAMS LISTCAT Cluster Output

Online Insertions

Online insertions must try to avoid CI/CA splits because the response time for all tasks accessing the dataset during a CI/CA split are affected. Whenever a split is being processed, the operations on the dataset are delayed until the split processing is completed. Enough free space should be available to keep splits to a minimum. If the dataset receives a lot of insertions, consider assigning this dataset to Non-Shared Resources (NSR) with additional data buffers so that the split could use chained I/O operations making the split processing faster.

For additional information review the following chapters:

- Chapter 3, Free Space
- Chapter 4, CI/CA Splits
- Chapter 9, CICS/VS

Online Access

Datasets that can be accessed online should have the proper buffering techniques applied. Datasets with low to medium activity should be placed into the Local Shared Resource (LSR) pool to reduce the amount of virtual storage required for processing. Datasets with high activity or that require chained I/O operations can be placed into NSR. With the improvement in the LSR buffer pool operations, high-activity datasets can be placed into the LSR pool, especially if placed into their own LSR pool. The proper selection of the number of strings or access paths and data/index buffers will affect the performance of the dataset. The CI size can also have a bearing on performance especially with small datasets that can be affected by requests for exclusive control. The CA size should be set to the maximum size possible in order to reduce the number of index records and possible levels. If the dataset can be equally distributed across several volumes, consider using KEYRANGES. Remember to place the indices in virtual storage to permit overlapped processing.

For additional information, review the following chapters:

- Chapter 2, Control Interval Size
- Chapter 4, CA Size
- Chapter 6, I/O Buffer Allocation
- Chapter 7, Space Allocation
- Chapter 8, Index Options
- Chapter 9, CICS/VS

Over Allocation

An area that must be continually analyzed, especially when new datasets are placed into production, is the amount of space allocated to the dataset. This is one area where many users have been able to recover DASD space and have deferred investments on additional units. The returning of unused space also has the effect of reducing the possibilities of fragmentation because more space has been returned to the pool. The allocation of space is sometimes problematic because incorrect calculations are made in determining the required space. The amount of space to be allocated can be controlled by using secondary allocations. In this manner, you can set the dataset to a lower allocation initially (primary) so that the loaded dataset would occupy between 90–95% of the primary space.

For additional information, review the following chapters:

- Chapter 2, Control Interval Size
- Chapter 3, Free Space
- Chapter 5, Control Area Size
- Chapter 7, Space Allocation
- Appendix A,, Reading an IDCAMS LISTCAT Cluster Output
- Appendix B, Computing VSAM Dataset Sizes

CI SPLITS

CI splits do not necessarily indicate that there is any cause for alarm. This is because CI splits are normally handled within the same cylinder. However, when the number of CI splits rises to a certain percentage of the total number of CAs, the user should be aware that a CA split may be about to occur. CI splits do cause extra overhead because two CIs must be written and extra space is available which may not be used. This means that when the dataset is read, two CIs must also be read for each CI split. As a result, the user should set a percentage guideline that, when exceeded, indicates that the dataset should be scheduled for reorganization.

For additional information, review the following chapters:

- Chapter 2, Control Interval Size
- Chapter 3, Free Space
- Chapter 4, CI/CA Splits

Critical Processing Window

Speed is an important factor whenever discussing critical windows. Most of the information stated in the section dealing with length of processing times applies here. In addition, the backup and restore process is also important in this process. The user should ensure proper buffering techniques for the VSAM datasets and a blocking factor close to 32K on the backup and restore device.

For additional information, review the following chapters:

- Chapter 2, Control Interval Size
- Chapter 3, Free Space
- Chapter 4, Control Area Size
- Chapter 6, I/O Buffer Allocation
- Chapter 7, Space Allocation
- Chapter 8, Index Options
- Chapter 10, Miscellaneous Considerations

Dataset Specifications

Several specifications can be counterproductive to the performance of the dataset. Users will have to evaluate the importance of these specifications in the environment. IMBED and REPLICATE can have an adverse effect on DASD space in return for faster access of the index records. Also, IMBED should not be specified for a dataset that occupies less than a maximum CA. RECOVERY is of no use in the dataset loading process unless the user has a routine that is prepared to handle the restart. If the dataset is loaded often, specify SPEED. ERASE is only of use when the dataset is being deleted. Unless the dataset requires heavy security, using this parameter makes the delete process slower. SHAREOPTIONS 4 forces a read for every record and associated index record. Unless the dataset actually requires this option, do not specify it.

For additional information, review the following chapters:

- Chapter 8, Index Options
- Chapter 9, CICS/VS Considerations
- Chapter 10, Miscellaenous Considerations

Over Allocation Free Space

As mentioned earlier, an excessive amount of FREESPACE can have a negative effect on the dataset performance. In particular, don't specify any free space value unless there are either additions or record lengthening operations. An incorrect specification elongates dataset processing times.

For additional information, review the following chapters:

- Chapter 2, Control Interval Size
- Chapter 3, Free Space
- Chapter 4, CI/CA Splits
- Chapter 10, Miscellaneous Considerations

Extra Extents

The objective when defining a dataset is to allocate one primary area of only one extent. Secondary allocations can be thought of as extensions to the process. The price paid for extra extents varies from extra virtual storage to having the dataset spread out on the disk unit(s). If the dataset is processed sequentially, there could be extra arm movement in going from one extent to the next. This should not be noticeable unless there are many extents. The main concern about extents is not the reading of the data after the extent is allocated, but when the actual extent allocation takes place. The file has to go through an "open" type sequence, which can affect the performance of the dataset. The user should gauge how fast the dataset is adding extents. If this occurs frequently, a dataset reorganization should be performed, with a review of the primary and secondary request units for the dataset.

The other area where extra extents can cause a degradation in the dataset is in the index area. Since the indices are written out sequentially in a flat dataset, any extra extents will cause arm movement in trying to locate the correct index record.

For additional information, review the following chapters:

- Chapter 2, Control Interval Size
- Chapter 4, CI/CA Splits
- Chapter 5, Control Area Size
- Chapter 10, Miscellaenous Considerations

CONCLUSION

The process to tuning VSAM datasets involves many apects, some of which are not directly associated with the VSAM datasets. The most important aspect of tuning VSAM datasets involves the user's knowledge of how VSAM datasets are organized and how they work. Most of the tuning work will go into the KSDS files.

Many third-party tools are available in the market that can mechanize this process for the user. However, it has been our experience that if the user understands what is involved in VSAM tuning, better use will be made of these tools. Without this knowledge the reader is blindly following recommendations that may not be effective for a given environment. The best tool is an understanding of the LISTCAT output. By being able to read this report, the reader can adjust any parameters that will improve the dataset's performance.

Appendix A
READING AN IDCAMS LISTCAT CLUSTER OUTPUT

The purpose of this appendix is to provide the user with sufficient information so as to be able to read a LISTCAT. Since these listings are extremely useful in dataset performance reviews, users should feel comfortable with a LISTCAT output. Only the important fields are reviewed.

A. CLUSTER

This area of the LISTCAT is used to identify the general information regarding the definition of a cluster. The name is the one provided by the user when the IDCAMS DEFINE is executed. Two fields are useful for tuning:

1. *CREATION* — This provides the date when this cluster was last reorganized. This date could be useful in determining the correct FREESPACE selection for the dataset.

2 *ASSOCIATIONS* — To identify all of the datasets that are related to this cluster. The user should evaluate all datasets mentioned here. Usually only the data and index (if present) are mentioned here. Alternate Indexes (AIX) are also mentioned.

B. DATA

This area provides the user with the information necessary to tune the data portion of the cluster. Several important fields are of use to the tuning process:

1. *ATTRIBUTES* — Used to define the characteristics assigned to the data through the DEFINE. The important subfields are:

   a. *KEYLEN* — provides the length of the key associated with the data. The size of the key is of particular importance as large keys are possible candidates for poor key compression. Keys over 20 bytes long are good suspects. RKP is the relative location of the key from the beginning of the record.

   b. *AVGLRECL/MAXLRECL* — provides the base for determining if the records are of variable- or fixed-length. If the average and the maximum record lengths are equal, the records are probably of fixed length; however, they could be shorter with no error indication given. The AVGLRECL is only used in space requirement computations when the space allocation is requested in RECORDS. Both of these lengths can also be important when determining the correct FREESPACE to be selected.

   c. *BUFSPACE* — provides the user with the total number of bytes allocated for data and, if present, index buffers. The default is two data and one index buffers.

   d. *CI SIZE* — provides the size of the unit of transfer between storage and the disk drive. It is an important tuning parameter since it affects the number of total I/O operations that may be required to process the dataset, and it is also used to determine the physical record size. The correct selection enhances not only processing time but also DASD space requirements.

e. *CI/CA* — specifies the number of CIs that will fit into the defined CA by the user space allocation request. VSAM adjusts the CA size to reflect the use of IMBED, which uses the first track track, or 62 FBA blocks, of each CA. This number is not adjusted to reflect the number of free CIs requested through the CA FREESPACE parameter. Therefore, the user must adjust this number in order to determine the actual number of usable CIs in the CA during the dataset load process. This number is used in the computation of the amount of space required to allocate a dataset.

f. *SHROPTNS* — this parameter specifies dataset sharing options for intra- and inter-system sharing. This parameter is important in the dataset integrity area. SHROPTNS 4 has a negative effect on dataset performance and should be well justified if used.

g. *SPEED/RECOVERY* —unless the user has a means of restarting a load from the point of abend, this parameter should specify SPEED. This will avoid the need to preformat each CA during the load process, thus making it faster. Be careful, RECOVERY is the default.

h. *SUBALLOC/UNIQUE/NOALLOC* — specifies the type of space allocation requested by the user in this parameter. UNIQUE datasets (non-ICF catalogs) only have a maximum of 16 extents per volume. NOALLOC is only available in DOS and is used in combination with the REUSE parameter to create dynamic files. ICF catalogs reflect UNIQUE for the VSAM datasets but still have 123 extents available.

i. *INDEXED/NONINDEXED/NUMBERED/NONVSAM* — KSDS/ESDS/RRDS specification. NONVSAM is none of the above.

j. *WRITECHK/NOWRITECHK* — specifies if the DASD verify feature is to be used after every write for the dataset. As the WRITECHK process requires at least one additional DASD revolution adversely affecting performance, NOWRITECHK is recommended. Remember that a CI can span several tracks depending on the device and definition.

k. *IMBED/NOIMBED* — IMBED specifies that the user has requested that the sequence set index records be placed with its corresponding CA. The sequence set record occupies the first track, or 62 FBA blocks, (3370) of the CA and the record is repeated (REPLICATE) the number of times that it will fit into the track, or 62 FBA blocks. An important area to watch when IMBED is specified is the CA size. IMBED should not be specified for a dataset that occupies less than one cylinder, or 744 FBA blocks. In these cases, the CA size should be specified as large as possible.

l. *REPLICATE/NOREPLICAT* — REPLICATE is used to indicate to VSAM that all index records (sequence and index set) are to be assigned an individual track, or 62 FBA blocks, and are to be repeated as many times as each index record fits into the track, or 62 FBA blocks. The user should watch that IMBED and REPLICATE are used together. If IMBED is not specified when REPLICATE is specified, the user is paying the price for extra DASD space for the sequence set without obtaining potential benefits of reduced access motion that could be obtained when IMBED is specified.

m. *ORDERED/UNORDERED* — used to control the sequence of volumes to be assigned when ORDERED is specified. This is important if the user is going to use KEYRANGES.

n. *REUSE/NOREUSE* — the combination of REUSE with NOALLOC (DOS only) provides the user with a dynamic dataset that will only occupy space when the dataset is opened and will return the space when the dataset is closed. Specifying REUSE for a dataset forces the dataset's HIGH-USED-RBA (HURBA) to be reset to zero (beginning of the dataset) when the dataset is opened for output. The use of REUSE limits the number of extents on one volume to 16.

o. *SPANNED/NONSPANNED* — used to indicate if spanned record support is desired for this dataset through using this parameter. The use of spanned records allows a logical record to exceed the size of a CI. If incorrectly specified, SPANNED can create a lot of unused space because each new record is aligned on a CI boundary.

2 *STATISTICS* — To describe the quantitative information about the data portion. These statistics are an important factor in the tuning process. The important subfields are:

a. *REC-TOTAL* — represents the total number of records in the dataset. This field is useful in determining the total space required for the dataset.

b. *REC-DELETED* — represents the total number of records that have been deleted from the dataset. This field is useful in helping determine the FREESPACE requirement.

c. *REC-INSERTED* — represents the total number of records that have been added to the dataset since the last reorganization. This total is useful in determining the FREESPACE requirement.

d. *REC-UPDATED* — represents the total number of updated records. If the records are of variable length, this field could be used to indirectly measure the total updates that could have received a record length change.

e. *REC-RETRIEVED* — represents the total number of accessed records. This number could be used in conjunction with the number of execute channel programs (EXCPs) to determine the number of EXCPS required by each operation. Too high a ratio could be indication of a small CI size or improper buffering.

f. *SPLITS-CI* — represents the total number of CI splits that have occurred since the last reorganization. This field can be used to evaluate the effectiveness of the FREESPACE allocated to the dataset. This type of split is not as critical as the CA split; however, it does provide an indication as to when to start expecting a CA split. The larger the number, the more the user should consider reorganizing the dataset to avoid a CA split. This is especially true if the dataset receives additions online. Also, a lot of unusable space may have been created.

g. *SPLITS-CA* — represents the total number of CA splits occurring since the last reorganization. This field can be used to evaluate the effectiveness of the FREESPACE allocated to the dataset. This value serves as a guide as to when the dataset should be reorganized. As in the case of CI splits, each CA split may have a lot of unusable space associated with it.

h. *FREESPACE %CI* —represents the amount of FREESPACE requested within a CA for a dataset at this time. It could have been modified by means of an IDCAMS ALTER command.

i. *FREESPACE- %CA* — represents the amount of FREESPACE requested within a CA for a dataset at this time. It could have been modified by means of an IDCAMS ALTER command.

j. *FREESPC-BYTES* — represents the total number of bytes available in completely free CIs in the dataset. This number can be used to determine if the key compression is not working well. This field represents the total number of free CIs in the dataset. An exceptionally high number can be an indication of poor key compression. The user will have to account for the free CIs created as a result of the FREESPACE CA% request, which is included in the FREE-SPACE-BYTES total. Also, this field can be used to determine if the dataset has been overallocated in space.

k. *EXCPS* — represents the number of Execute Channel Programs that have been requested for this dataset. This statistic, in combination with the record statistics (TOTAL, DELETED, INSERTED, UPDATED, and RETRIEVED) can be used to determine if proper buffering has been allocated and if the CI sizes are adequate. A high EXCP count to total records RETRIEVED can point to inadequate buffering of the data for sequential processing. The way to use this number and the record statistics is to issue a LISTCAT before processing the dataset, and another immediately after processing the dataset. The difference in record total statistics and EXCP counts can be used to determine the total number of EXCPs per access.

l. *EXTENTS* — represents the number of DASD extents that this dataset has allocated to it. If this number is greater than one immediately after a load, it should be investigated. This can mean one of the following:

   1) The primary space requested was too low.

   2) The primary space was adequate but the key compression was poor, leaving many unused CIs in the allocated CAs.

   3) The disk space is fragmented and large chunks of contiguous space may not be available.

   All of these conditions merit a review of the cluster definition unless the file is very large and occupies more than one volume. In this case, the user may have wanted a smaller space allocation to avoid an overallocation on the secondary volume(s). Multiple extents can have an effect on sequential dataset processing if extents already exist. If additional extents are being created, slow processing can occur since "open" type logic is being performed against the dataset.

m. *SYSTEM-TIMESTAMP* — represents the time of last activity on the dataset. This is printed in Time of Day (TOD) clock format. Unless a conversion routine is available, this field is not of much use.

3. *ALLOCATION* — to describe the general details of "how" the space for the dataset was allocated and used.

   a. *SPACE-TYPE* — represents "how" the user requested space. Three options can appear here: CYLINDERS, TRACKS or BLOCKS. Space requested in RECORDS is converted to one of these. This parameter is useful in determining the CA size.

   b. *SPACE-PRI* — represents the amount of space requested by the user for the primary allocation.

   c. *SPACE-SEC* — represents the amount of space requested by the user for the secondary allocation.

   ***************************NOTE******************************

   The PRIMARY and SECONDARY allocations are used by VSAM to determine the CA size. Follow the rules established in Chapters 1 and 5 in allocating the largest CA size possible. An allocation in CYLINDERS will ensure a maximum CA size for Count Key Data disk units. An allocation in multiples of 744 blocks will ensure a maximum CA size for Fixed Block Architecture disk units.

   ****

   d. *HI-ALLOC-RBA* — represents the highest allocated byte address for the dataset, including the primary and all secondary allocations. VSAM treats any dataset as if it were one continuous virtual storage.

e. *HI-USED-RBA* — represents the highest byte address used by the dataset. This field, in combination with the HI-ALLOC-RBA, can be used to determine if either too much or too little space has been allocated for the dataset and how much space is left to the end of the dataset.

4. *VOLUMES* —— to identify the physical characteristics of the dataset. The physical areas and volumes assigned are also identified. The more important subfields are:

a. *VOLSER* — identifies all the volumes allocated to the dataset. All volume serial numbers that contain data or have been identified as alternates (CANDIDATES) are listed in this area. If the volume is actually used, more information is provided such as the extents of where the data is located. This information is valuable in the distribution of data across several volumes.

b. *DEVTYPE* — identifies the device type being used. In DOS, the actual device type is printed. In MVS, a code is used to represent the device type. Some of the device type codes are as follows:

1) 3000 8001	9 Track Tape
2) 3040 200A	3340 (35M/70M)
3) 3050 2006	2305-1
4) 3050 2007	2305-2
5) 3050 2009	3330 (MOD 1 or 2)
6) 3050 200B	3350
7) 3050 200D	3330-11
8) 3010 200C	3375
9) 3010 200E	3380

c. *PHYREC-SIZE* — represents the actual physical record size that has been selected for the CI size stated above. The idea is to make the physical record size equal the CI size. MVS uses multiples of .5, 1.0, 2.0 and 4.0K as the base for determining the physical record size (PRE-DFP V2.3). DOS does not use this technique and therefore can create a physical record size of up to 8K. This can create some compatibility problems. Small physical record sizes for larger CI sizes can be detrimental to DASD performance. FBA devices do not have this problem because the FBA block size is 512 bytes, which is always a multiple of the CI size. Any space loss on the FBA unit will occur at the end of the CA.

d. *PHYRECS/TRACK* — represents the number of physical records that can be written on one track. To determine how many CIs this represents, the user must determine how many physical records are required for one CI. This is done by dividing the CISIZE by the PHYSREC-SIZE. The result can now be used as the divisor into PHYSREC/TRACK in order to determine the number of CIs per track. Remember that CIs can span tracks but cannot span CAs. Therefore, the more important value will be determined using the next field.

e. *TRACKS/CA* — provides the user with the size selected by VSAM to serve as the CA size for the dataset. As stated above, the objective is to have the largest CA size possible up to the maximum CA size. If this size is not as large as it should be, revise the primary and secondary allocation requests. For FBA devices, this field is BLOCKS/CA.

f. *HI-ALLOC-RBA/HI-USED-RBA* — to identify (through repetition by volume) which parts of the RBAs fall into the particular volume being listed.

g. *EXTENTS* — provided by VSAM for each extent allocated on this volume the LOW-CCHH/HIGH-CCHH and equivalent LOW-RBA/HIGH-RBA for the dataset. The cylinder and head number can be used to list the dataset if required, as this indicates where the data portion lays physically on the volume. For FBA devices, substitute BLOCKS for CCHH above.

h. *TRACKS* — informs how many tracks each extent contains. For FBA devices, substitute BLOCKS for tracks.

If the amount listed is not equivalent to the primary or the secondary values, DASD fragmentation has occurred. Fragmentation means that the requested amount could not be accommodated contiguously. VSAM will use up to five extents to allocate the requested amount. Multiple extents should be investigated as it could be an indication of incorrect allocation request or poor key compression.

C. INDEX

This area describes the characteristics for the index of a KSDS file. Most of the fields have already been discussed and will not be mentioned here. There are some important differences such as the applicability of RECOVERY to the index portion. The differences are covered individually.

1. *AVGLRECL/MAXLRECL* — The index record size is always seven bytes less than the CI size specified. AVGLRECL length is always zero.

2. *BUFSPACE* — The buffer allocation is specified in the DATA portion. The index BUFSPACE is always zero.

3. *CISIZE* — Normally, the index and data CI size will be different. If the index and data CISIZE are equal, check to make sure that the CISIZE was not specified at the cluster level instead of the data level. It is best to let VSAM select the index CI size, but caution must be observed for poor key compression. If the index CI size is larger than the data CI size, then it is possible that a small data CI size has been selected within a large CA size. Review the data CI size and make it larger if appropriate.

4. *RECOVERY* — The index always runs in recovery mode.

5. *INDEX LEVELS* — This number represents the number of index levels associated with this dataset. Any more than three levels is suspicious and should be investigated.

6. *HI-LEVEL-RBA* — This represents the RBA of the highest level index within the index area. This is where VSAM begins to scan for the location of a key.

7. *REC-TOTAL* — This field indicates the total number of index records associated with this KSDS file. It can be used to determine the number of sequence and index set records.

8. *EXTENTS* — Whenever IMBED is specified for the dataset, the index will reflect the extents of the data where the sequence set records are stored. The index area extents are also listed. The volume data is also printed.

Appendix B
COMPUTING VSAM DATASET SIZES

I. ESTIMATING THE SIZE OF A FIXED-LENGTH RECORD DATASET

Fixed-length datasets are relatively easy to compute space requirements. This section will provide some examples. The computed sizes are at 100% compaction. The user may want to increase the amounts by 5% or 10% to provide for growth.

1)	Total number of records	100,000	records
2)	Logical record length	1,000	bytes
3)	CI size	4,096	bytes
4)	CA size	1	cylinder (CASES A/B)
		744	blocks (CASES C/D)

CASE A. CKD WITH NO FREESPACE NOIMBED

1) Free space requested
   a) CI percentage 0 %
   b) CA percentage 0 %
2) NOIMBED/NOREPLICATE

Step 1.

Compute the imaginary free space line in the CI. Since no CI free space is requested, the entire CI is available for records.

Step 2.

Compute the number of logical records that fit into a CI. Since no CI free space is requested, the entire 4096 bytes less VSAM control information is available for the logical records. The records are of fixed length; only 10 bytes are necessary for VSAM control information (one CIDF and two RDFs).

CI size	4096	bytes
Minus VSAM control info.	-10	bytes
Total bytes for log. recs.	4086	bytes

Compute 4086 bytes/1000 bytes per logical record
RESULT ——————→ 4 Records per CI

(*Note:* There are 86 bytes remaining of fragmentation.)

Step 3.

Compute the number of CIs required to accommodate the data set.

Compute 100000 records/4 records per CI
RESULT ——————→ 25,000 CIs

Step 4.

a) Determine how many CIs/CA there are. The CI size is 4096 and this is a 3380 DASD unit; thus ten 4K records fit on a track. Each 3380 cylinder consists of 15 tracks.

Compute 15 tracks * 10 CIs per track
RESULT ——————→ 150 CIs per CA

b) Determine how many CIs would have been lost to IMBED. Since there is no IMBED, there is no loss.

c) Determine how many CIs/CA have been reserved for CA free space. Since no CA free space is requested, there is no CA free space.

d) Compute the total number of CIs available for data.

Compute	150 CIs/CA
Minus loss for IMBED	– 0 CIs/CA
Minus loss for CA Fspc.	– 0 CIs/CA
RESULT ——→	150 CIs/CA are available for data

Step 5.

Compute the number of CAs required for the dataset.

Compute	25000 CIs/150 CIs per CA
RESULT ——→	166.7 CAs

Step 6.

The total number of cylinders required to hold the dataset is 167. The number of CAs must be rounded up because you cannot allocate a partial CA.

CASE B. CKD WITH FREESPACE AND IMBED

1) Free space requested
   a) CI percentage 25 %
   b) CA percentage 10 %
2) IMBED/NOREPLICATE

Step 1.

Compute the imaginary free space line in the CI. A 25% CI free space was requested. Whenever CI free space is requested, the VSAM control must be subtracted, that is,

10 bytes for fixed-length records (one CIDF and two RDFs).

Compute 4096 – (4096 bytes* .25 – 10) (rounded down)
RESULT ——————→ Imaginary line at byte 3062

Step 2.

Compute the number of logical records that fit into a CI. The imaginary line is at byte 3062 and includes the VSAM control.

Compute 3062 bytes/1000 bytes per logical record
RESULT ——————→ 3 Records per CI

(*Note:* There are 62 bytes remaining of fragmentation.)

Step 3.

Compute the number of CIs required to accommodate the data set.

Compute 100000 records/3 records per CI (rounded up)
RESULT ——————→ 33,334 CIs

Step 4.

a) Determine how many CIs/CA there are. Since the CI size is 4096 and this is a 3380 DASD unit, ten 4K records fit on a track. Each 3380 cylinder consists of 15 tracks.

Compute 15 tracks * 10 CIs per track
RESULT ——————→ 150 CIs per CA

b) Determine how many CIs would have been lost to IMBED. Since IMBED is specified, the first track is lost. Since there are ten CIs per track, the loss would be 10 CIs.

c) Determine how many CIs/CA have been reserved for free space. Since a 10% CA free space is requested, the space reserved would be 14 CIs; the amount computed must take into account the IMBED specification (150 CIs minus IMBED amount of 10 CIs).

d) Compute the total number of CIs available for data.

Compute	150 CIs/CA
Minus loss for IMBED	– 10 CIs/CA
Minus loss for CA Fspc.	– 14 CIs/CA
RESULT ——————►	126 CIs/CA are available for data

Step 5.

Compute the number of CAs required for the dataset.

Compute	33334 CIs/126 CIs per CA
RESULT ——————————————►	264.6 CAs

Step 6.

The total number of cylinders required to hold the dataset is 265. The number of CAs must be rounded up because you cannot allocate a partial CA.

(*Note:* Specifying IMBED and CI/CA free space increases the total space required for the dataset by almost 100 cylinders.)

CASE C. FBA WITH NO FREESPACE AND NOIMBED

1) Free space requested
   a) CI percentage 0 %
   b) CA percentage 0 %
2) NOIMBED/NOREPLICATE

Step 1.

Compute the imaginary free space line in the CI. Since no CI free space is requested, the entire CI is available for records.

Step 2.

Compute the number of logical records that fit into a CI. Since no CI free space is requested, the entire 4096 bytes less VSAM control information is available for the logical records. As the records are of fixed length, only 10 bytes are necessary for VSAM control information (one CIDF and two RDFs).

CI size	4096	bytes
Minus VSAM control info	– 10	bytes
Total bytes for log. recs.	4086	bytes

Compute 4086 bytes/1000 bytes per logical record

RESULT ——————————► 4 Records per CI

(*Note:* There are 86 bytes remaining of fragmentation.)

Step 3.

Compute the number of CIs required to accommodate the data set.

Compute 100000 records/4 records per CI

RESULT ——————————► 25,000 CIs

Step 4.

a) Determine how many CIs/CA there are. The CI size is 4096 and this is a 3370 DASD unit. Each 4K CI requires 8 FBA blocks. The 3370 CA consists of 744 blocks.

Compute 744 blocks per CA/8 FBA blocks per CI
RESULT ⟶ 93 CIs per CA

b) Determine how many CIs would have been lost to IMBED. Since there is no IMBED, there is no loss.

c) Determine how many CIs/CA have been reserved for CA free space. Since 0 CA free space is requested, there is no loss.

d) Compute the total number of CIs available for data.

Compute	93 CIs/CA
Minus loss for IMBED	– 0 CIs/CA
Minus loss for CA Fspc.	– 0 CIs/CA
RESULT ⟶	93 CIs/CA are available for data

Step 5.

Compute the number of CAs required for the dataset.

Compute 25000 CIs/93 CIs/CA
RESULT ⟶ 268.8 CAs

Step 6.

The total number of blocks required to hold the dataset is 200,136. The number of CAs must be rounded up because you cannot allocate a partial CA. This number is then multiplied by 744 blocks to determine the total number of blocks required for the dataset.

CASE D. FBA WITH FREESPACE AND IMBED

1) Free space requested
   a) CI percentage 25 %
   b) CA percentage 10 %
2) IMBED/NOREPLICATE

Step 1.

Compute the imaginary free space line in the CI. A 25% CI free space was requested. Whenever CI free space is requested, the VSAM control must be subtracted, that is, 10 bytes for fixed-length records (one CIDF and two RDFs).

Compute 4096 – ((4096 bytes* .25 – 10) (rounded down)
RESULT ——————→ Imaginary line at byte 3062

Step 2.

Compute the number of logical records that fit into a CI. The imaginary line is at byte 3062 and includes the VSAM control.

Compute 3062 bytes/1000 bytes per logical record
RESULT ——————→ 3 Records per CI

(*Note:* There are 62 bytes remaining of fragmentation.)

Step 3.

Compute the number of CIs required to accommodate the dataset.

Compute 100000 records/3 records per CI
RESULT ——————→ 33,334 CIs

Step 4.

a) Determine how many CIs/CA there are. The CI size is 4096 and this is a 3370 DASD unit. Each 4K CI requires 8 FBA blocks. The 3370 CA consists of 744 blocks.

Compute 744 blocks per CA/8 FBA blocks per CI
RESULT ——————→ 93 CIs per CA

b) Determine how many CIs would have been lost to IMBED. Since IMBED is specified, the first 62 blocks are lost. This means that only 682 blocks are available in the CA. Therefore,

Compute	682 blocks per CA/8 FBA blocks per CI
RESULT ———→	85 CIs per CA

(*Note:* 2 FBA blocks or 1K are lost to fragmentation. The total loss including IMBED is 8 CIs or 64 FBA blocks.)

c) Determine how many CIs/CA have been reserved for CA free space. Since 10% CA free space is requested, the space available is 9 CIs (DOS/VSE rounds up).

d) Compute the total number of CIs available for data.

Compute	93 CIs/CA
Minus loss for IMBED	– 8 CIs/CA
Minus loss for CA Fspc.	– 9 CIs/CA
RESULT ———→	76 CIs/CA are available for data

Step 5.

Compute the number of CAs required for the dataset.

Compute	33334 CIs/76 CIs per CA
RESULT ———→	451.8 CAs

Step 6.

The total number of blocks required to hold the dataset is 336,288. The number of CAs must be rounded up because you cannot allocate a partial CA. This number is then multiplied by 744 blocks to determine the total number of blocks required for the dataset.
(*Note:* The difference of IMBED and CI/CA free space increases the total space required for the dataset by almost 136,000 FBA Blocks.)

II. ESTIMATING THE SIZE OF A VARIABLE-LENGTH RECORD DATASET

It is more complicated to compute the amount of space required for variable-length datasets. The main reason is because of the VSAM control information which is also variable. This section provides some examples that can be of use in determining the size of the dataset. The computed sizes are at 100% compaction. The user may want to increase the amounts by 5% or 10% to provide for growth.

1)	Total number of records	100,000	records
2)	Logical record length	650	bytes (average)
		1,000	bytes (maximum)
3)	CI size	4,096	bytes
4)	CA size	1	cylinder (CASES E/F)
		744	blocks (CASES G/H)

CASE E. CKD NO FREESPACE AND NOIMBED

1) Free space requested
   a) CI percentage 0 %
   b) CA percentage 0 %
2) NOIMBED/NOREPLICATE

Step 1.

Compute the imaginary free space line in the CI. Since no CI free space is requested, the entire CI is available for records.

Step 2.

a) If the length distribution is known for the dataset by number of records within each length, prepare a similar chart using the length for distribution:

Length	# of Records	Total Bytes
200	2000	400000
500	4000	2000000
650	86000	55900000
1000	8000	8000000
	TOTAL BYTES	66300000

b) If the length distribution is not known, use the average record length in the following computation:

Compute 100000 records * 650 bytes average length
RESULT ——————————► 65000000 Total Bytes

(*Note:* The key to use is the record length that occurs most often or in the statistical "mode" of the dataset. This normally provides a good estimate unless there is an even distribution of lengths. In this case, the average or mean would be the best.)

c) Compute the number of logical records that fit into a CI. As there is no CI free space requested, the entire 4096 bytes less VSAM control information is available for the logical records. As the records are variable length, an estimate as to the number of RDFs will have to be made. There is no formula available for determining the number of RDFs. However, based on our average record length of 650 bytes and the CI size of 4096 bytes, we can determine that, at best case, were all the record lengths the same, we could only fit 6 records per CI and would leave around 196 bytes of fragmentation. So, if we said that the worst case would be each record having its own RDF, then we would be using 18 bytes for the RDFs and 4 bytes for the CIDF. The total would be 22 bytes.

CI size	4096	bytes
Minus VSAM control info	– 22	bytes
Total bytes for log. recs.	4074	bytes

Compute 4074 bytes/650 bytes per logical record
RESULT ——————————— 6 Records per CI
(*Note:* There are 174 bytes remaining of fragmentation.)

Step 3.

Compute the number of CIs required to accommodate the dataset.

Compute 100000 records/6 records per CI
RESULT ———————————→ 16,667 CIs

Step 4.

a) Determine how many CIs/CA there are. Since the CI size is 4096 and this is a 3380 DASD unit, ten 4K records fit on a track. Each 3380 cylinder consists of 15 tracks.

Compute 15 tracks * 10 CIs per track
RESULT ———————————→ 150 CIs per track

b) Determine how many CIs would have been lost to IMBED. Since there is no IMBED, there is no loss.

c) Determine how many CIs/CA have been reserved for CA free space. Since no CA free space is requested, there is no loss.

d) Compute the total number of CIs available for data.

Compute	150 CIs/CA
Minus loss for IMBED	– 0 CIs/CA
Minus loss for CA Fspc.	– 0 CIs/CA
RESULT ———————→	150 CIs/CA are available

Step 5.

a) Compute the number of CAs required for the dataset.

Compute	16667 CIs/150 CIs/CA
RESULT ——→	111.1 CAs

b) For verification, the computations made in Step 2a or 2b can be used. There is no need to use both figures. The largest one will be sufficient. In this case, it will be 2a.

1) Compute	6 records per CI * 650 average length
RESULT ——→	3900 bytes usable per CI
Compute	150 CIs/CA * 3900 bytes per CI
RESULT ——→	585000 bytes usable per CA
Compute	66300000 bytes in file/585000 bytes per CA
RESULT ——→	113.3 CAs required

Step 6.

The total number of cylinders required to hold the dataset is 114. The number of CAs must be rounded up because you cannot allocate a partial CA. Use the higher amount as a hedge against any miscalculation.

CASE F. CKD WITH FREESPACE AND IMBED

1) Free space requested
   a) CI percentage 25 %
   b) CA percentage 10 %
2) IMBED/NOREPLICATE

Step 1.

Compute the imaginary free space line in the CI. A 25% CI free space was requested.

Compute   4096 – (4096 bytes* .25) (rounded down)
RESULT ——————→ Imaginary line set at byte 3072

Step 2.

a) If the length distribution is known for the dataset by number of records within each length, prepare the following chart:

Length	# of Records	Total Bytes
200	2000	400000
500	4000	2000000
650	86000	55900000
1000	8000	8000000
	TOTAL BYTES	66300000

b) If the length distribution is not known, use the average record length in the following computation:

Compute   100000 records * 650 bytes average length
RESULT ——————→ 65000000 Total Bytes

(*Note:* The key to use is the record length that occurs the most often or statistical mode in the dataset. This normally provides a good estimate unless there is an even distribution of lengths. In this case, the average or mean would be the best.)

c) Compute the number of logical records that fit into a CI. Since CI free space is requested, 3072 bytes of usable space including VSAM control information is available for the logical records. As the records are of variable length, an estimate as to the number of RDFs will have to be made. There is no formula available for determining the number of RDFs. However, based on our average record length of 650 bytes and the CI size of 3072 bytes, we can determine that, at best, all the record lengths were the same; we could only fit 4 records per CI, leaving around 472 bytes of free space. So, if we said that the worst case would be each record having its own RDF, we would be using 12 bytes for the RDFs and 4 bytes for the CIDF. The total would be 16 bytes.

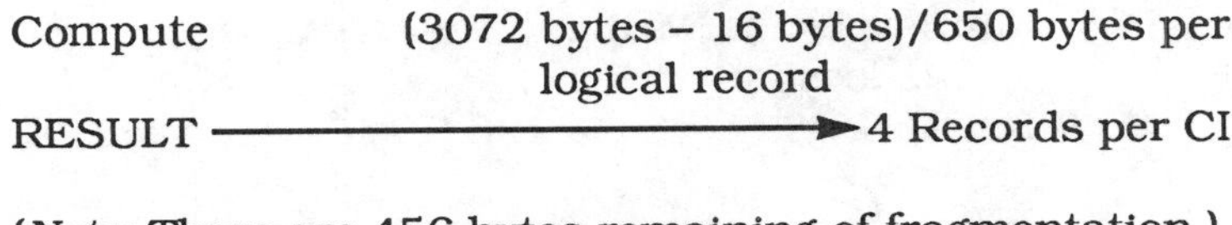

Compute
(3072 bytes – 16 bytes)/650 bytes per logical record
RESULT
4 Records per CI

(*Note:* There are 456 bytes remaining of fragmentation.)

Step 3.

Compute the number of CIs required to accommodate the data set.

Compute 100000 records/4 records per CI (rounded up)

RESULT ——→ 25,000 CIs

Step 4.

a) Determine how many CIs/CA there are. Since the CI size is 4096 and this is a 3380 DASD unit; ten 4K records fit on a track. Each 3380 cylinder consists of 15 tracks.

Compute 15 tracks * 10 CIs per track

RESULT ——→ 150 CIs per CA

b) Determine how many CIs would have been lost to IMBED. Since IMBED was specified, the first track would be lost. Since there are 10 CIs per track, the total loss would be 10 CIs.

c) Determine how many CIs/CA have been reserved for CA free space. Since a 10% CA free space is requested, the space reserved would be 14 CIs (150 CIs minus IMBED amount of 10 CIs).

d) Compute the total number of CIs available for data.

Compute	150 CIs/CA
Minus loss for IMBED	– 10 CIs/CA
Minus loss for CA Fspc.	– 14 CIs/CA
RESULT ——→	126 CIs/CA are available for data

Step 5.

a) Compute the number of CAs required for the dataset.

Compute	25000 CIs/126 CIs/CA
RESULT ——→	198.4 CAs

b) For verification, the computations made in Step 2a or 2b can be used. There is no need to use both figures. The largest one will be sufficient. In this case, it will be 2a.

1) Compute	4 records per CI * 650 average length
RESULT ——→	2600 bytes usable per CI
2) Compute	126 CIs/CA * 2600 bytes per CI
RESULT ——→	327600 bytes usable per CA
3) Compute	66300000 bytes in file/327600 bytes per CA
RESULT ——→	202.4 CAs required

Step 6.

The total number of cylinders required to hold the dataset is 203. The number of CAs must be rounded up because you cannot allocate a partial CA. Use the higher amount as a hedge against any miscalculation.

CASE G. FBA WITH NO FREESPACE AND NOIMBED

1) Free space requested
   a) CI percentage 0 %
   b) CA percentage 0 %
2) NOIMBED/NOREPLICATE

Step 1.

Compute the imaginary free space line in the CI. Since no CI free space is requested, the entire CI is available for records.

Step 2.

a) If the length distribution is known for the dataset by number of records within each length, prepare the following chart.

Length	# of Records	Total Bytes
200	2000	400000
500	4000	2000000
650	86000	55900000
1000	8000	8000000
	TOTAL BYTES	66300000

b) If the length distribution is not known, use the average record length in the following computation:

Compute 100000 records * 650 bytes average length
RESULT ———————————— 65000000 Total Bytes

(*Note:* The key is to use the record length that occurs most often or the statistical mode in the dataset. This normally provides a good estimate unless there is an even distribution of lengths. In this case, the average or mean would be the best.)

c) Compute the number of logical records that fit into a CI. Since no CI free space is requested, the entire 4096 bytes less VSAM control information is available for the logical records. As the records are of variable length, an estimate as to the number of RDFs will have to be made. There is no formula available for determining the number of RDFs. However, based on our average record length of 650 bytes and the CI size of 4096 bytes, we can determine that, at best, all the record lengths were the same; we could only fit 6 records per CI and would leave around 186 bytes of fragmentation. So, if we said that the worst case would be each record having its own RDF, we would be using 18 bytes for the RDFs and 4 bytes for the CIDF. The total would be 22 bytes.

CI size	4096	bytes
Minus VSAM control info	– 22	bytes
Total bytes for log. recs.	4074	bytes

Compute 4074 bytes/650 bytes per logical record

RESULT ——————————► 6 Records per CI

(*Note:* There are 174 bytes remaining of fragmentation.)

Step 3.

Compute the number of CIs required to accommodate the data set.

Compute 100000 records/6 records per CI

RESULT ——————————► 16,667 CIs

Step 4.

a) Determine how many CIs/CA there are. Since the CI size is 4096 and this is a 3370 DASD unit, 8 FBA blocks are required per record. The CA size is 744 blocks.

Compute 744 blocks/8 FBA blocks per logical record
RESULT ——————————→ 93 CIs/CA

b) Determine how many CIs would have been lost to IMBED. Since there is no IMBED, there is no loss.

c) Determine how many CIs/CA have been reserved for CA free space. Since 0% CA free space is requested, there is no loss.

d) Compute the total number of CIs available for data.

Compute 93 CIs/CA
Minus loss for IMBED − 0 CIs/CA
Minus loss for CA Fspc. − 0 CIs/CA
RESULT ——————→ 93 CIs/CA are available for data

Step 5.

a) Compute the number of CAs required for the dataset.

Compute 16667 CIs/93 CIs/CA
RESULT ——————————→ 179.2 CAs

b) For verification, the computations made in Step 2a or 2b can be used. There is no need to use both figures. The largest one will be sufficient. In this case, it will be 2a.

1) Compute 6 records per CI * 650 average length
RESULT ——————→ 3900 bytes usable per CI

2) Compute 93 CIs/CA * 3900 bytes per CI
RESULT ——————→ 362700 bytes usable per CA

3) Compute 66300000 bytes in file/362700 bytes per CA
RESULT ——————→ 182.8 CAs required

Step 6.

The total number of blocks required to hold the dataset is 136,152. The number of CAs must be rounded up because you cannot allocate a partial CA. The amount has to be multiplied by 744 blocks in a CA to find the number of blocks required for the dataset. Use the higher amount as a hedge against any miscalculation.

CASE H. FBA WITH FREESPACE AND IMBED

1) Free space requested
   a) CI percentage 25 %
   b) CA percentage 10 %
2) IMBED/NOREPLICATE

Step 1.

Compute the imaginary free space line in the CI. A 25% CI free space was requested.

Compute 4096 – (4096 bytes* .25) (rounded down)
RESULT ————→ Imaginary line set at byte 3072

Step 2.

a) If the length distribution is known for the dataset by number of records within each length, prepare the following chart.

Length	# of Records	Total Bytes
200	2000	400000
500	4000	2000000
650	86000	55900000
1000	8000	8000000
	TOTAL BYTES	66300000

b) If the length distribution is not known, use the average record length in the following computation:

Compute 100000 records * 650 bytes average length
RESULT ——————————► 65000000 Total Bytes

(*Note:* The key is to use the record length that occurs most often or the statistical mode in the dataset. This normally provides a good estimate unless there is an even distribution of lengths. In this case, the average or mean would be the best.)

c) Compute the number of logical records that fit into a CI. Since CI free space is requested, 3072 bytes of usable space including VSAM control information is available for the logical records. Since the records are of variable length, an estimate as to the number RDFs will have to be made. There is no formula available for determining the number of RDFs. However, based on our average record length of 650 bytes and the CI size of 3072 bytes, we can determine that, at best, all the record lengths were the same; we could only fit 4 records per CI and would leave around 472 bytes of free space. So, if we said that the worst case would be each record having its own RDF, we would be using 12 bytes for the RDFs and 4 bytes for the CIDF. The total would be 16 bytes.

Compute (3072 bytes – 16 bytes)/
650 bytes per logical record
RESULT ——————————► 4 Records per CI

(*Note:* There are 456 bytes remaining of fragmentation.)

Step 3.

Compute the number of CIs required to accommodate the dataset.

Compute 100000 records/4 records per CI
RESULT ——————————► 25,000 CIs

Step 4.

a) Determine how many CIs/CA there are. Since the CI size is 4096 and this is a 3370 DASD unit, 8 FBA blocks are required per record. The CA size is 744 blocks.

Compute 744 blocks/8 FBA blocks per logical record
RESULT ——————→ 93 CIs per CA

b) Determine how many CIs would have been lost to IMBED. Since IMBED was selected, the first 62 FBA blocks are lost. This would mean that there are only 682 blocks available in the CA. Therefore,

Compute 682 blocks per CA/8 FBA blocks per CI
RESULT ——————→ 85 CIs/CA are available for data

(*Note:* 2 FBA blocks or 1K would be lost to fragmentation. The total loss would be 8 CIs.)

c) Determine how many CIs/CA have been reserved for CA free space. Since a 10% CA free space is requested, the space reserved would be 8 CIs.

d) Compute the total number of CIs available for data.

Compute	93 CIs/CA
Minus loss for IMBED	– 8 CIs/CA
Minus loss for CA Fspc.	– 8 CIs/CA
RESULT ——————→	77 CIs/CA are available for data

Step 5.

a) Compute the number of CAs required for the dataset.

Compute 25000 CIs/77 CIs/CA
RESULT ——————→ 324.7 CAs

b) For verification, the computations made in Step 2a or 2b can be used. There is no need to use both figures. The largest one will be sufficient. In this case, it will be 2a.

1) Compute 4 records per CI * 650 average length
   RESULT ——————► 2600 bytes usable per CI

2) Compute 7 CIs/CA * 2600 bytes per CI
   RESULT ——————► 200200 bytes usable per CA
3) Compute 66300000 bytes in file/200200 bytes per CA

   RESULT ——————► 331.2 CAs required

Step 6.

The total number of blocks required to hold the dataset is 247,008. The number of CAs must be rounded up because you cannot allocate a partial CA. This number must be multiplied by 744 blocks per CA to determine the number of blocks required for the dataset. Use the higher value as a hedge against any miscalculation.

Appendix C
REFERENCE MANUALS

This is a brief list of IBM reference manuals that may be of use to the reader.

FORM NO.	TITLE
GG24-1563	*VSAM Primer for the Integrated Catalog Facility in a MVS Environment*
G320-5774	*VSAM Primer and Reference*
GA26-1661	*3880 Storage Control Description*
GA26-1638	*3350 DASD Storage Reference Guide*
GA26-1657	*3370 DASD Description*
GA26-1666	*3370 DASD Storage Description and User's Guide*
G221-2455	*3370 DASD Models A2, B2, A12, and B12*
GA26-1664	*3380 DASD Storage Description and User's Guide*
GC226-4193	*3380 DASD Models AD4, BD4, AE4, and BE4-G.I.*
GC26-3838	*OS/VS VSAM Programmers Reference Manual*
GC26-3841	*OS/VS2 AMS*
GC26-4015	*MVS/XA VSAM Administration Guide*

GC26-4019	*MVS/XA ICF Administration: AMS*
GC26-4041	*MVS/XA Catalog Administration*
SC24-5144	*Using VSE/VSAM Command and Macros*
SC24-5145	*VSE/VSAM Programmer's Reference*

Appendix D
TUNING USING A LISTCAT

Tuning is not an easy process when using an output from IDCAMS LISTCAT because a LISTCAT does not provide a user-friendly output. In fact, a LISTCAT ALL can be fairly voluminous in the number of pages printed, making the listing cumbersome to read. Due to this, many third-party software products have been made available to help in the tuning of VSAM datasets. However, it is our experience that to be effective in using these third-party software packages, the user should first learn how to tune VSAM *without* the software tool. Most of these software tools are not necessarily well documented and do not explain the reasoning regarding the recommendations developed. Following some of the recommendations blindly can sometimes be more problematical than not taking any action at all. In this appendix we discuss a step-by-step approach toward tuning a VSAM dataset using a LISTCAT.

As you become more familiar with VSAM, modify the procedure to suit the best needs of the installation. It is imperative to remember previous specifications for the dataset as you go through these steps. Only by associating the different parameters can the correct tuning process be developed. The terminology used is explained in the book. The steps are:

1. Locate the dataset(s) to be tuned in the LISTCAT output. If no specific dataset(s) are selected, proceed with the next steps for each dataset in the LISTCAT.

2. Verify the creation date of the dataset. This date is given in a Julian format. This date is important in the determination of free space allocated and when to reorganize the dataset.

3. Based on the cluster's name or other information such as the size of the dataset (number of records, space allocated, or dataset importance to the installation), you should be able to initially determine if this is a primary dataset requiring attention or if this dataset should be put off after all the primary files have been tuned. The important principle here is to spend time initially on those datasets that are going to have a good return on investment (ROI).

4. Having selected an important dataset, the first area to analyze is the dataset's attributes. Several things should be analyzed in this area. As a matter of reference, study the dataset's key length. Any key over 20 bytes is a candidate for poor key compression. This may not be visible at this point. The following fields or specifications should be analyzed:

   a) Average/Maximum Record Length: These figures will also be used in determining the effect of fragmentation in the CI and in the amount of allocated space required to hold this dataset. When the average and the maximum reflect the same size, the dataset should be of fixed length. This may not be necessarily true as VSAM will accept record lengths of less than the maximum as valid. When the lengths are different, the user can think of the dataset as being of variable length. Again, this may not be true because we could write out the entire dataset using the same length. Use of the record length to compute dataset sizes is explained in Appendix B.

5. The CI size of the data should be analyzed. The first analysis should be to compare the CI length to the physical record size. The objective is to have these two sizes equal each other. If the sizes are unequal, a review of the CI size is in order. The following questions should be answered:

a) Was the data CI size specified in the cluster definition or was VSAM requested to select the CI size?

b) Does the CI size reflect an unblocked format? Does this dataset require this? Is this a protected dataset?

c) Is the data and index CI size equal? Was the CISZ parameter specified at this cluster definition level?

A good data CI size for most I/O devices and types of processing (direct or sequential) is 4K. This size is also good for paging operations. Deviations from this figure can be a result of logical record size and CI fragmentation. In general terms, the CI and physical record size provide the best results when equal in size, except when the CISZ is larger than the operating system generated maximum physical record length.

6. An area that is closely related to the data (and index) CI size is the buffer space reserved. If the VSAM default is taken, this figure should reflect twice the data CI size plus index CI size, if present. Normally the default is fine because this size can be altered in several ways. A greater specification may be provided as in the case of alternate indices, which are accessed through the path in an online environment. The preferred method is to alter this amount temporarily through the JCL (// DD or // DLBL).

7. Certain parameters should be reviewed to ensure that they were correctly specified.

   a) RECOVERY: This is the default. Unless the user has a recovery routine, the user should specify SPEED to avoid preformatting the CAs.

   b) ERASE: This parameter should only be specified for highly confidential datasets that require the elimination (erasure) of the data when the dataset is deleted. If this is not the case, deletion of the dataset can take longer due to the clearing of the DASD space.

c) WRITECHK: This parameter is used to indicate to VSAM that every record written should be reread. This requires at least one additional disk rotation, making the total time to write the record longer than normal. As discussed in Chapter 10, this parameter should only be specified under special conditions. Unwarranted use can be detrimental to performance.

d) IMBED/REPLICATE: Normally these two features should be specified together. Avoid using REPLICATE without IMBED. These options should not be used if virtual/real storage is available and/or DASD space is at a premium. IMBED should never be specified for a dataset that has a CA size of less than the Max-CA size; the user should make the Max-CA equal to the maximum that can be specified by making the primary and secondary allocations equal to create a one-level index composed of one-sequence set index record. In addition, if IMBED is specified, the CA-size should be equal to the Max-CA size to avoid DASD space waste.

e) SHROPTNS: Avoid the use of SHAREOPTIONS 4, which negates any buffer performance options.

f) REUSE/UNIQUE: Be aware that both of these specifications reduce the total number of extents for VSAM datasets (Non-ICF) to 16 per volume versus 123. Datasets created under the ICF structure appear as UNIQUE but still can have up to 123 extents.

g) SPANNED: Should only be specified if necessary because more DASD space could result if incorrectly specified.

8. A review of the dataset statistics is an important process in tuning a VSAM dataset. Among the fields to be analyzed are:

a) CI/CA Splits: If splits are present, reorganization may be necessary. This can be due to either the extra extents created by CA splits or the unusable space created by the splits. In addition, datasets with splits should have a certain amount of free space (FSPC) allocated at either the CI or CA level.

b) Free Space Allocation: Be sure that there are records inserted (or expanded) in order to justify any percentage in this area. If there are no insertions and/or expansion, be sure that the percentage is set to zero.

c) EXTENTS: When initially loading the dataset, the total number of extents should equal one. Any deviation from this figure can indicate a poor primary selection, that the DASD does not have sufficient contiguous space, poor key compression, or that the user forced this allocation. Whenever multiple extents exist immediately after loading the dataset, the user should investigate the reasons for the multiple extent allocation.

d) EXCPs: This measurement can be used to determine if the CI size and/or buffer allocations are set correctly. Too high a proportion between I/O requests and total records accessed/updated/deleted/added can reflect a poor CI size or poor buffer allocation selection.

9. The amount of space requested for the dataset is very important. Too much space can result in wasted space which other datasets cannot use. Too little space can result in multiple extents causing unnecessary "open" overhead processing. These situations can be measured using the high allocated and high used values combined with the free space bytes. If too much space is allocated, this space should be returned to the pool. If too little space is allocated, the primary allocation should be increased.

10. The number of tracks per CA should be set to the Max-CA for all datasets that exceed one cylinder, or 744 FBA blocks. If there is any dataset that is less than the Max-CA, the value should be set to the maximum size possible to reduce the number of CAs and therefore reduce the number of sequence set index records. IMBED should not be specified for a dataset that is less than the Max-CA size.

The preceding procedure illustrates many options that must be analyzed by the person tuning the VSAM datasets. Many of these parameters are interrelated and require additional information to make a decision. It is imperative that the person performing the tuning be aware of the uses and requirements of the VSAM datasets being tuned.

Appendix E
VSAM SPACE CALCULATION

I. COMPUTING SPACE

The relationship between the CI size and physical record size is important in determining the DASD capacity. We will discuss this topic using CKD units. DOS and MVS use different criteria in this area. DOS can write a physical record that varies in size from 512 bytes to 8192 bytes. These physical records include intermediate sizes, depending on the DASD devices used. MVS (NONDFP 2.3), on the other hand, only has four physical record sizes to use. These are 512, 1024, 2048, and 4096 bytes. Therefore, it is possible to obtain different DASD capacities when using the same CI size in DOS and MVS. This is caused by DOS trying to use the CI size as the physical record size (intermediate) while MVS uses the largest multiple of the CI size using the four record sizes available to MVS. For example, for a CI size of 1536 bytes DOS on some devices will try to write a physical record of 1536 bytes. For the same situation, MVS (Non DFP and DFP 2.2 and earlier) will write three physical records of 512 bytes. As can be seen, the total DASD utilization per track will vary by operating system and device.

MVS DFP 2.3 will try to use the CISZ selected as the physical record size unless this results in poor track utilization. CIs can span across tracks but cannot span past CA boundaries. Therefore, if there is any unused space, it will occur at the end of the CA. A CA can be as small as one track and as large as one cylinder. The size of the track and number of tracks per cylinder vary by the DASD unit used. The number of physical records per track varies by the size used. The total number of physical records written per CA varies by the size of the CA. The physical record size can be found in the LISTCAT under the title PHYREC-SIZE. The number of times that this physical record will fit on a track can be found under PHYRECS/TRK; the CA size can be found under TRACKS/CA. Thus the total number of physical records that can be written in a CA is the multiplication of the fields PHYRECS/TRK times TRACKS/CA.

Formula 1. Computing the number of physical records per CA.

*Number of Physical Records per CA = PHYRECS per Track * Tracks*

This does not necessarily represent the number of CIs/CA, especially if the physical record and CI sizes are not equal. To determine how many physical records are required per CI, take the CI size and divide it by the physical record size. There can be no remainder. A result of one will reflect that the CI and physical record sizes are equal. Any other result indicates the number of physical records required to make a CI.

Formula 2. Computing the number of physical records per CI.

Number of Physical Records per CI = CISZ / PHYREC-SIZE.

If you take the number of physical records per CA calculated above and divide it by the number of physical records per CI, you will get the number of CIs per CA. Any remainder from this division is lost. This is the fragmentation that can occur at the end of a CA. Note that IMBED reduces the total number of tracks available for data in a CA by one.

Formula 3. Computing the number of CIs per CA.

$$\text{Number of CI per CA} = \frac{\text{Number of Physical Records per CA}}{\text{Number of Physical Records per CI}}$$

Normally a LISTCAT provides this information for you. However, if a LISTCAT is not available, the user must compute these values.

Each CA has the same size throughout the dataset. That is, the data portion CA is the same size throughout the data portion. In a KSDS, the index CA size can be different from the data CA size. The index CA size, however, must be constant throughout the index portion. This rule applies to both the primary and secondary allocations of the dataset. Each CA has the same number of CIs and contains the same number of bytes. Each CI within the CA is the same size. To determine the number of bytes in a CA, multiply the CI size by the number of CIs/CA. This figure will be used in determining the number of free CAs left in the dataset.

Formula 4. Computing the number of bytes per CA.

*Number of Bytes per CA = CISZ * Number of CIs per CA.*

The figure at HI-ALLOC-RBA represents the total number of bytes allocated to the dataset. This figure is equivalent to the multiplication of the number of primary allocation CAs times the number of bytes per CA plus any secondary allocation CAs times the number of bytes in a CA. As the dataset is loaded, the dataset is allocated by CA. The sum of all the used CAs is called the HI-USED-RBA.

Formula 5. Computing the number of CAs in the Dataset.

$$\text{Number of CAs in the Dataset} = \frac{\text{HI-ALLOC-RBA}}{\text{Number of Bytes per CA}}$$

The difference between the HI-ALLOC-RBA and the HI-USED-RBA represents the number of bytes left from the last used CA (which contains the end of file) to the end of the allocated space.

Formula 6. Computing the number of available bytes left in the dataset.

Number of Available Bytes Left in the Dataset = HI-ALLOC-RBA — HI-USED-RBA.

If you take this difference and divide it by the number of bytes per CA, you will know the number of free CAs available for dataset extension or CA splits.

Formula 7. Computing the number of free CAs.

$$\text{Number of Free CAs} = \frac{\text{Number of Available Bytes Left in the Dataset}}{\text{Number of Bytes per CA}}$$

The specification in FRESPC-BYTES reflects the number of completely free CIs within the dataset. This includes all CIs reserved through the FREESPACE CA percentage, all free CIs following the EOF markers until the end of the allocated space, and most important, all free CIs left in control areas due to poor key compression.

II. PROCEDURE FOR DETERMINING THE DATASET SPACE

The following procedure can be used to determine the size of the dataset space required on the DASD unit for the file. The formulas depend on having a LISTCAT of a model dataset. The best way is to define a one-cylinder dataset (or less if you want the allocation in tracks), issue a LISTCAT and a delete the dataset. The values in this model can be used to compute the space required.

Step 1. Compute the number of logical records per CI.

If the logical record is fixed length, then:

$$\text{Number of Recs per CI} = \frac{\text{Data CI Size} - ((\text{Data CI Size} * \%\ \text{CI FSPC}) - \text{VSAM CTL})}{\text{Logical Record Length}}$$

where:

Data CI Size	=	the selected data CISZ of the DEFINE cluster.
% CI FSPC	=	the percentage to be used in reserving free space at the CI level.
VSAM CTL	=	the total number of bytes of control information within a CI. If unblocked, use 7 bytes. If fixed blocked, use 10 bytes.
Logical Record Length	=	length of the average record in the dataset.

If the logical record is variable length, then:

$$Number\ of\ Recs\ per\ CI = \frac{(Data\ CI\ Size - 4) - (Data\ CI\ Size * \%\ CI\ FSPC))}{(Logical\ Record\ Size + 3)}$$

(*Note:* The number of records per CI is rounded down in either case.)

Step 2. Compute the number of CIs available for data in CA.

*Number of Data CIs per CA = Number of CIs per CA – (Number of CIs per CA * % CA FSPC)*

(*Note:* The product of % CA FSPC and number of CIs per CA is rounded down for MVS/XA. For DOS (VSE/SP), this product is rounded up.)

Step 3. Compute the number of records per CA.

*Number of Records per CA = Number of Records per CI * Number of Data CIs per CA*

Step 4. Compute the number of CAs required for the dataset.

$$\textit{Number of CAs in Dataset} = \frac{\textit{Total Number of Records in Dataset}}{\textit{Number of Records per CA}}$$

Step 5. Compute the number of tracks or cylinders in the dataset.

*Number of Tracks in Dataset = Number of Trks per CA * Number of CAs in dataset*

$$\textit{Number of Cylinders for Dataset} = \frac{\textit{Number of Trks in Dataset}}{\textit{Number of Trks per Cylinder}}$$

where:

3330	=	19 Tracks/Cylinder	
3340	=	12 Tracks/Cylinder	(Includes 3344)
3350	=	30 Tracks/Cylinder	
3375	=	12 Tracks/Cylinder	
3380	=	15 Tracks/Cylinder	
3390	=	15 Tracks/Cylinder	

(*Note:* Round up number of cylinders for dataset.)

The examples given in Appendix A use a similar technique.

III. PROCEDURE FOR COMPUTING NUMBER OF SEQUENCE AND INDEX SET RECORDS (KSDS)

Step 1. Compute total of number of bytes per CA.

Data CISZ × Number of CIs per CA = Total Number of Bytes per CA

where:

- Data CISZ is from LISTCAT.
- Number of CIs/CA is from LISTCAT.

- Total Number of Bytes per CA is total number of bytes available for data (including FSPC CIs) in a CA.

Step 2. Compute total number of CAs (used) in the dataset.

$$\frac{\textit{HI-USED-RBA}}{\textit{Total Number of Bytes/CA}} = \textit{Total Number of Used CAs (Sequence Set Records) in File}$$

where:

HI-USED-RBA is from LISTCAT.

(*Note:* If HI-ALLOC-RBA is used, you will compute the total number of CAs allocated for the dataset).

- Total Number of Bytes/CA is computed in part A.

- Total Number of Used CAs in File is the result from the formula.

(*Note:* This is an important figure because this represents the total number of sequence set records.)

Step 3. Determine Number of Index Set Records.

Index Record Total – Total Number of Sequence Set Records = Total Number of Index Set Records

where:

- Index Record Total is from LISTCAT.

- Total Number of Sequence Set Records is computed in Step II.

- Total Number of Index Set Records is remaining number of records represents the Index Set.

Step 4. Determine Number of Index Set Records by Index Level.

(*Note:* You will always have *only one* record at the highest index level. The remainder of the index set records represents the level(s).)

Determine the number of index levels in the dataset; this information is available in the LISTCAT.

- If one level, the result in Step III should be zero.
- If two levels, the result in Step III should be one.
- If three levels, subtract 1 from the total in Step III. This is to remove the high-level index. The remainder is the number of index set records in the second level.
- If four or more levels, there is no direct method of determining the number of index set records in the intermediate levels. It is probable that you will only have two index set records at the second highest level. This means that if you subtract 3 from the total, the remainder should be the number of lowest level index set records. However, this has to be a very large dataset to have four levels. Verify the CI size and data CA size to ensure that they are specified correctly.

IV. DETERMINING THE AVERAGE RECORD LENGTH

Determining the average record length may not be an easy process if an automated tool is not available. The average record length is used by VSAM whenever determining the amount of space to allocate when the user requests space in RECORDS in the cluster. One simple method of estimating the average record length is by taking the HI-USED-RBA from LISTCAT immediately after loading the dataset and dividing it by the number of records in the dataset. This will yield a slightly higher average length, especially if CI and CA free space is specified. The amount of space fragmentation (implicit CI free space) will also increase the size of the average record length.

If free space is specified, the amount reserved will have to be backed out of the HI-USED-RBA. This process involves determining the amount of free space reserved in each CI as well as the number of free CIs per CA. The number of free CIs/CA should be multiplied by the number of CAs in the dataset. This product should be subtracted from the HI-USED-RBA. The amount reserved for CI free space can be easily determined by multiplying the data CI size free space percentage. With this information, the user can also determine the amount of free space left due to fragmentation.

The total amount of free space in the CI is the sum of the explicit (% FSPC * Data CI Size) and implicit (fragmentation) free space. This total can now be multiplied by the number of usable CIs in a CA (i.e., total CIs/CA minus free space CIs). This gives you the total amount of free space per CA. This total must now be multiplied by the number of CAs in the dataset. This product must also be subtracted from the HI-USED-RBA. The remainder is the net bytes used, which can be divided by the number of records in the dataset to determine the average record length.

This procedure is effective for fixed-length records. For variable-length records, an estimate of the fragmentation space must be made. A slightly longer average record length will not be as bad as a shorter amount. The preceding procedure will be effective for variable-length records even if the fragmentation is ignored.

Glossary

Access Method Services (AMS). This is a set of utilities available to the user to work with VSAM datasets and catalogs. Through the use of the comprehensive utility package, the user can define datasets, catalogs, and VSAM spaces. Other functions available include the deletion and alteration of dataset definitions. A set of utilities available permit the printing, storing, and loading functions. The program is called IDCAMS. Some portions can work with non-VSAM datasets.

AIX. This refers to an alternate index dataset.

ALTER command. This command is available under IDCAMS and can be used to change some of the current definitions for the dataset.

Alternate index. This is a dataset that allows the user to access another dataset through a secondary key. The cluster that contains the secondary keys is called an alternate index cluster, whereas the one containing the primary key is called the base cluster.

Average rotational delay. This is the time taken on average for a desired record to come under the read/write mechanism. Most estimates (i.e., those that don't take device, control unit, or channel busy into consideration) take the minimum amount (0 milliseconds) and add it to the maximum amount. This total is divided by two to determine the average. The maximum amount varies by disk unit. This time is also called "latency."

Average seek time. This is the time that it takes the read/write mechanism to cover one-third of the cylinders on the disk unit.

Backup. This is the process where the contents of a dataset are copied to another media so as to provide the capability of re-creating the dataset if something were to occur to the original file.

CA. *See* Control Area.

Catalog. This is a special type of dataset used by different access methods to hold information regarding user datasets or files and other catalogs. See *also* master catalog, user catalog, and Integrated Catalog Facility (ICF).

CI. *See* Control Interval.

CIDF. *See* Control Interval Definition Field.

CKD. An abbreviation for Count-Key-Data devices such as the IBM 3330 or 3380 disk units.

Control area. This is one of the building blocks of a VSAM dataset. It is composed of a series of control intervals and is commonly referenced as a CA. For Count-Key-Data (CKD) devices, a CA can range from a minimum of one track to as large as a cylinder. For Fixed Block Architecture (FBA) devices, a CA can range from a minimum of 62 FBA blocks to a maximum of 744 FBA blocks.

Control area split. This is a process that occurs only on KSDS files whenever a record is added or expanded and there is no more room available within the control interval causing a control interval split. To accommodate this control interval split, there has to be a free CI within the CA. If none is available, a control area split occurs. In this process, a certain number of the original CIs are moved or split to a new CA, which is acquired at the end of the dataset.

Control interval. This is the basic unit of transfer between the disk and main storage. The size of the CI varies from a minimum of 512 bytes, to a maximum of 32K bytes. The CI size will vary in increments of 512 bytes until 8K and then in increments of 2K until 32K.

Control interval definition field. This field consists of four bytes and is located at the end of all CIs. It is used by VSAM to control the location and amount of free space left in the CI.

Control interval split. This is a process that occurs only on KSDS files when a record is added or expanded and there is a room available within the control interval to accommodate the record. To accommodate it, the control interval is divided into two or more CIs with a part of the records moved to a new CI within the remainder staying in the original CI (those records with lower key values).

Cylinder. This is a term used to describe the number of tracks that can be accessed with a single positioning of the read/write mechanism. It can be thought of as a concentric number of tracks. The number of tracks in a cylinder varies by device. For example, an IBM 3350 has 30 tracks to a cylinder, whereas an IBM 3380 has 15 tracks to the cylinder.

DASD. *See* Direct Access Storage Device.

Data component. This is the part of the dataset that describes the data records.

Data Facility/Extended Functions. An IBM utility that is a prerequisite for an ICF environment. This facility enhances certain VSAM functions.

Data Facilities Product. An IBM utility used to create an ICF environment and enhances certain VSAM functions.

Dataset. Another name for a file. It is a collection of related records.

DEFINE command. The command used to allocate or create datasets, spaces, user/master catalogs, paths, and alternate indices.

DELETE command. The means used to eliminate things created by the DEFINE command.

DFP. *See* Data Facilities Product.

Direct access. This refers to the process of obtaining a record from a disk unit without having to read all the intervening records.

Direct Access Storage Devices. This is another name for a disk drive.

Entry. One or more records in a VSAM/ICF catalog that contains information about a dataset.

Entry name. This refers to the datasets in the catalog.

Entry Sequence Dataset. This is one of the organizations available under VSAM, which is used whenever the records in the file are accessed and/or created by physically writing one record after the other. The records may or may not be in logical sequence.

ESDS. *See* Entry Sequence Dataset.

Extent. This refers to the space which is allocated to a file on the disk unit.

Free space. This is the amount of space left over in either a CI or a CA that is currently not being used by records. This free space may be allocated by the user through the use of the FSPC parameter in the cluster definition (explicit definition) or it can be allocated as a result of imperfect record fits into a CI (implicit definition). Free space may occur as a result of CI or CA splits.

Generic key. This is a partial key in which the significant characters are left justified and the remaining characters are padded, usually with low- values (X'00') or spaces (X'40'). The subject of the full key is used to locate a particular starting point on the dataset. It is used in skip sequential type processing.

Horizontal pointer. This is a pointer available in the index records to point to the next index record at the same level. It is important at the sequence set level when the dataset is being read sequentially because the next logical index record can be found without going back to the higher level index set records to follow the pointers downward (vertical pointers).

ICF. *See* Integrated Catalog Facility.

IIP. *See* ISAM Interface Program.

Index component. This is the part of the dataset that describes the index records. It is usually independent of the data component except when IMBED is specified for the file. In this case, part of the index component (sequence set) resides with the data component.

Index entry. A catalog entry for an index.

Index set. This is the collective name by which all indices above the sequence set are known.

Integrated Catalog Facility. This is a modern catalog facility available for users who have the DF product.

ISAM Interface Program. This term describes a series of emulation programs that give the user the capability of running unaltered ISAM programs to access VSAM datasets. These routines are also called IIP.

Key. A field within the record that defines the record in the file. In the case of the base cluster, the key must be unique. In the case of alternate keys, nonunique keys are allowed.

Key compression. A technique used by VSAM to shorten the length of the key that must be carried in the index records. VSAM will use front key compression by eliminating that part in the front of the key that is repetitive in nature in comparison to the previous key. VSAM will use rear key compression by eliminating that part of the key that contains nonsignificant characters when compared to the next key. The value of this algorithm is that space is saved in the index record.

Key sequence. This is used to specify the order in which the records are accessed from a dataset. The value used is the record's key instead of the record's location.

Key Sequence Dataset. This is a form of VSAM organization that provides the capability to access records in logical sequence while allowing access to any record directly.

KSDS. *See* Key Sequence Dataset.

Latency. *See* Average Rotational Delay.

LISTCAT command. This command lists one or more catalog entries pertaining to the datasets and associated volumes defined and controlled by the catalog.

Master catalog. This term describes the principal catalog to the operating system. This catalog can either be a VSAM catalog, as in the case of DOS and MVS (non ICF), or an ICF catalog, as in the case of MVS ICF. This catalog is assigned at IPL time.

MBBCCHHR. This is an area in storage that is used to identify the physical disk address being accessed. It is a discontinuous binary number. M is the extent number. BB is used to identify the bin cell to be used by an IBM 2321 Data Cell which is obsolete. These bytes are binary zero. CC identifies the cylinder number. HH selects the head (track). R identifies the record number on the track.

Nonunique key. This is a secondary key found in an AIX dataset which does not have to unique. An example of this type of key could be when the name is used as an index. In this case, the same name could refer to several other unique keys.

Path. A dataset used to access records from a base cluster through an alternate index.

Physical record. This term describes the actual record being written on the disk unit. The length of the physical record written may be different from the CI size described for the file.

Pointer. A key or an address used to locate a CI or a record in a dataset.

Primary space allocation. This is the amount of space requested for a dataset when it is first created. It refers to the first amount specified in the CYLINDERS, TRACKS, BLOCKS, or RECORDS parameter of the AMS DEFINE command.

Primary key. This is the unique record identification in a dataset.

PRINT command. This command is available to the user to list records in a VSAM dataset.

RBA. *See* Relative Byte Address.

RDF. *See* Record Definition Field.

Record Definition Field. This is a three-byte field, which is used by VSAM internally to control the length of the record associated with it. The RDFs are written starting from an adjacent position to the CIDF in a right to left manner. The data records that are represented by these RDFs are stored in a left to right manner. Whenever two or more contiguous records of the same size exist in the data, VSAM will couple two RDFs to reflect all the data records of the same size. The first RDF contains the length, whereas the second RDF contains the number of times that this length should be repeated. For RRDS files, there is one RDF per slot in the CI.

Relative Byte Address. The displacement of a CI or record from the beginning of the file. VSAM looks at a dataset as though it were one contiguous storage beginning at zero and extending to the total sum of all the CI lengths in the file.

Relative Record Dataset. This is another VSAM organization where the records are loaded into fixed-length slots. The relative slot position from the beginning of the dataset becomes the relative number for the slot. It is through this relative record number that a record can be accessed.

Relative Record Number. An integer that describes the relative position of a slot from the beginning of the file.

Reorganization. This is the process where the dataset is unloaded to another device and then restored. This process is usually associated with KSDS files to get the file back into some form of physical sequence, which may have been lost through CA splits.

REPRO command. This all-purpose utility command can be used to make copies of part or all of a file and to load them back.

Reusable dataset. This is a dataset that has its HI-USED-RBA reset back to zero whenever the dataset is opened for output. This resetting logically deletes any records that were in the dataset before the open occurred.

Rotational delay. This is the amount of time required for a disk unit to complete one entire revolution under the read/write mechanism.

Rotational Position Sensing. This is a hardware feature that can be used to lower channel utilization. This is accomplished by sending a sector number to the DASD control unit which will release the channel while the disk unit waits for the particular sector to come near the read/write mechanism.

RPS. *See* Rotational Position Sensing.

RRDS. *See* Relative Record Dataset.

RRN. *See* Relative Record Number.

Search time. This is the amount of time spent by a disk unit waiting for the correct record identifier (CCHHR) or key to come under the read/write mechanism. During this process, the channel is busy.

Secondary space request. This is the second amount that can be specified in the definition of a dataset. This amount refers to the amount of disk space that is to be allocated to the file whenever the dataset gets full and runs out of DASD space. This quantity can be specified in the CYLINDERS, TRACKS, BLOCKS, or RECORDS parameter of the AMS DEFINE command.

Seek time. The amount of time it takes the read/write access mechanism to reach the desired location (BBCCHH) on a disk drive.

Sequence set: This is the lowest level of indices available to a KSDS file. Each sequence set record contains the high key values of each CI in a CA. There is one sequence set index record per used CA.

Shared DASD. Disk units that can be accessed by more than one CPU.

Index

A

B

H

I

J

K

L

M

N

O

P

R

S

T

U

V

W